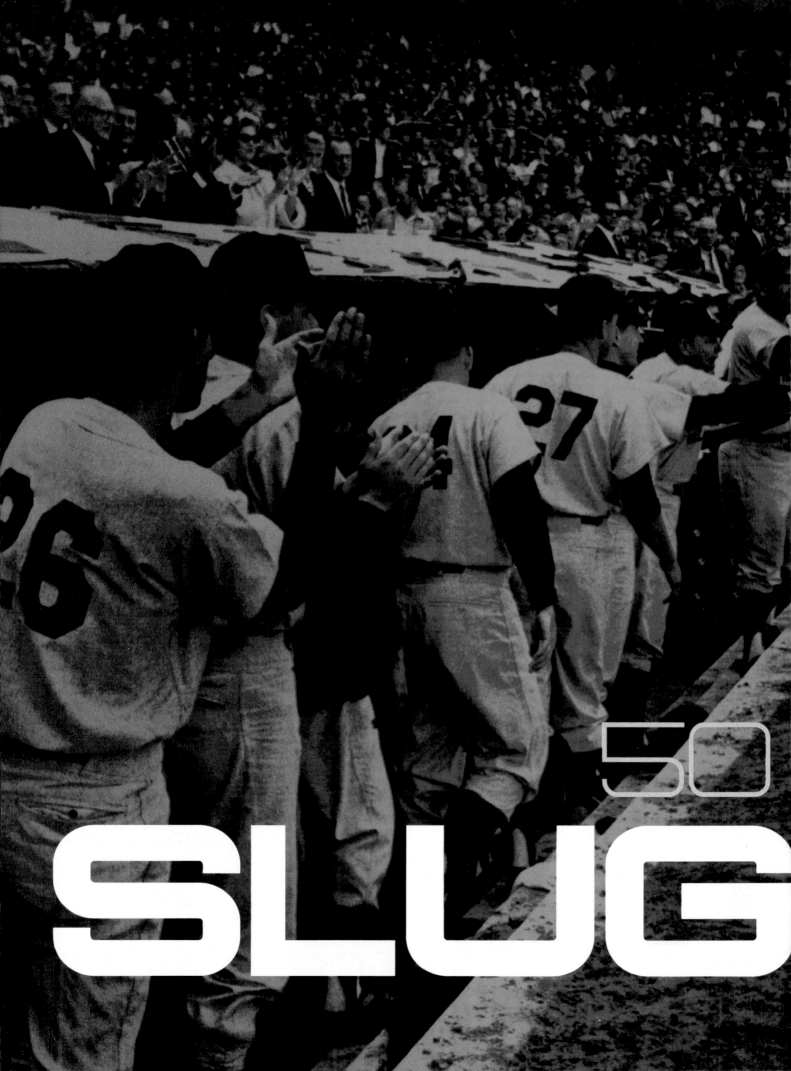

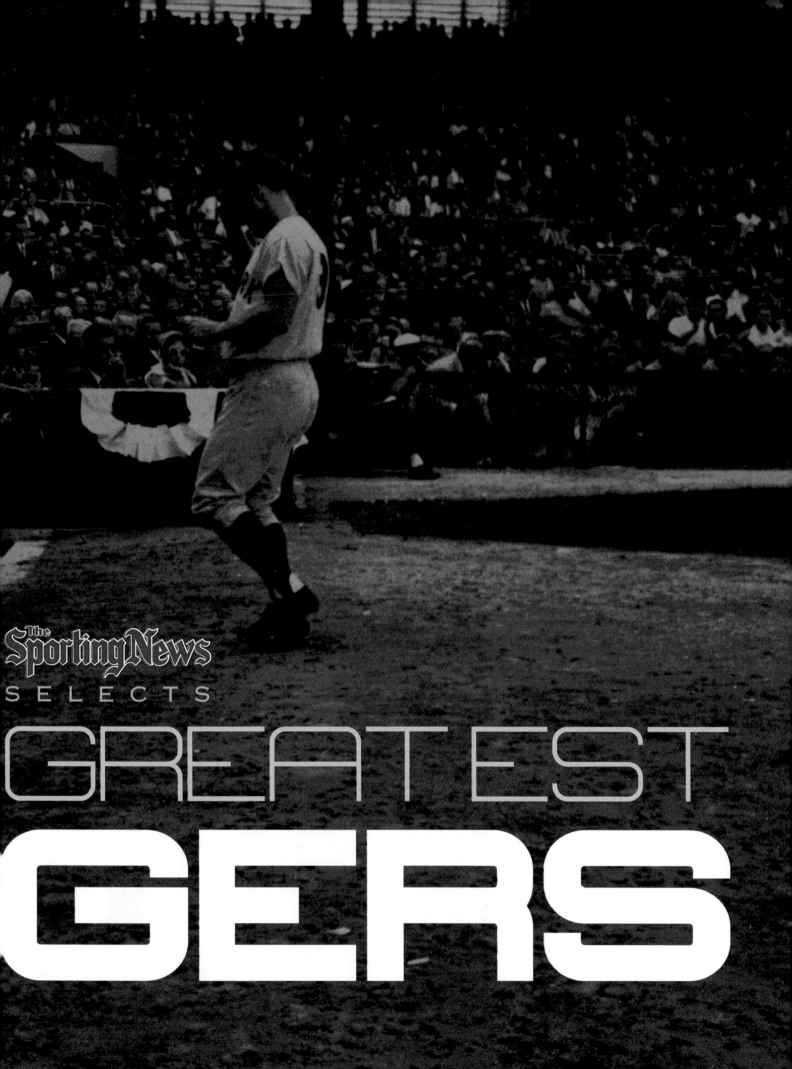

The Sporting News
SELECTS

GREATEST
GERS

CONTENTS

Ted Kluszewski, 1954

TION

In Babe Ruth's day,

manager Miller Huggins explained it this way: "Fans like the fellow who carries the wallop."

In Ralph Kiner's time, a teammate said: "Home run hitters drive Cadillacs. Singles hitters drive Fords."

In the late-1990s, pitcher Tom Glavine lamented to teammate Greg Maddux in a television commercial: "Chicks dig the long ball."

Different times. Different eras. Different ways of saying the same thing.

When it comes to captivating American baseball fans, nobody does it quite like the game's sluggers. Pitching may be 75 percent of the game, but the fraction reserved for those who hit it further than anybody else get the disproportionate share of fan interest and attention—not to mention salary.

It's no coincidence that with every spike in offense throughout the 20th century, attendance jumped along with it. And when it comes to run production, singles, doubles and stolen bases are nice, but nothing changes a game faster than a three-run homer.

"People just like to see things big," slugger Reggie Jackson says. "Big houses. Big cars. Big money."

And big flies. It's been that way ever since Ruth put the home run on the map and slugged himself into international stardom. Argue all you want about the social impact of Muhammad Ali and Jesse Owens, but no athlete in the 20th century changed his sport more than Babe Ruth.

And there is no underestimating the positive effect modern-day sluggers Mark McGwire and Sammy Sosa had on the game during their stirring and touching pursuit of Roger Maris' home run record in the 1998 season. Just four years ear-

Babe Ruth put the home run on the map in the 1920s, while Reggie Jackson glamorized the long ball in the 1970s. And each of them did it in a Yankee uniform.

lier, the game was in dire straits, crippled by a players strike that led to the only cancellation of the World Series.

But that and the game's other problems took a back seat to those two sluggers, men from dramatically different backgrounds but with the same penchant for hitting majestic home runs. The Cardinals' McGwire capped it off by hitting No. 69 and No. 70 in Busch Stadium on the final day of the season, setting a new standard that seems as unreachable as Babe Ruth's 60 once did, and then Maris' 61, which stood for 37 years.

And what did McGwire have to say for himself? "What I've accomplished is fabulous. I'm riding the wave, along with America. I'm like in awe of myself right now. I'm speechless, really. I can't believe I did it. Can you?"

Neither could his manager, Tony La Russa: "It's even stranger than fiction, what this man has done and become."

If hitting a baseball is the hardest thing to do in sports—as Ted Williams says and many agree—than just how must it feel to propel baseballs 400-plus feet? And how do they do it?

"You can't describe that kind of thing to a guy that's never done it," says Jackson, who did it 563 times in regular-season play. "Ninety percent of the home runs you hit out of the ballpark, you know they're gone. You feel contact, but you know it's sweet. You know it's perfect. It's bat speed. It's strength. It's timing. It's lower body. And then the weight of the bat helps, too. If you don't have the strength, you can't use a big bat."

In other words, sluggers are a very small fraternity. And that's what makes them special. It was about the time Mickey Mantle was sending momentous clouts out of parks around the American League in the late 1950s and early 1960s that the term tape-measure home run was coined, and distances began to be measured in rudimentary fashion.

Now, with the aid of advancing technologies, stadiums around the game have every square inch

Just four years after baseball had put itself in dire straits and canceled the World Series, Mark McGwire and Sammy Sosa brought the game back with their stirring pursuit of Roger Maris' record. McGwire broke it, and hit his 69th and 70th on the last day of the 1998 season, setting a new standard.

of home run territory beyond outfield fences calculated for distance from home plate. A slugger sends one into orbit, and almost before he is around the bases, the distance the ball traveled is posted on the scoreboard. Sports highlight shows only feed the monster, playing and replaying the blasts over and over each night.

As the first baseball season of the new millennium unfolds, what better time to look back on the history and evolution of slugging—to name names and list the deeds of the game's top fifty sluggers, to place their accomplishments into the perspective of the game around them and to trace how their methods and equipment have changed over the years. And who knows—maybe what we learn here will help us identify the next Ruth and McGwire and Griffey and Mantle ...

The names Roger Maris (below) and Mickey Mantle are indelibly linked not only in Yankee lore but in baseball history. It was their stirring pursuit of Babe Ruth in the summer of '61 that captivated a nation.

"There will never be another guy like the Babe. **I get more kick ou**

Momentous clouts

Where to begin? How about No. 60 in 1927, off Tom Zachary in Yankee Stadium. It was the milestone for all sluggers to shoot at for 33 years. His longest may have come on June 8, 1926, when his blast out of Detroit's Navin Field came to rest about 623 feet from home plate. Did he call his shot against Charlie Root in the 1932 World Series? And what better way to go out than with his final three homers—all on the same day in Forbes Field, with the latter estimated at 600 feet.

1

BABE
RUTH

On the day of Ruth's funeral, sportswriter Tommy Holmes said to Red Smith, "Some 20 years ago, I stopped talking about the Babe for the simple reason that I realized that those who had never seen him didn't believe me."

6-2, 215 Career HRs: 714 Career slugging percentage: .690 HR-to-hit ratio: 1 to

Home Runs/Slugging%
* led league

Year	HR	SLG	Year	HR	SLG	Year	HR	SLG
1914	0	.300	1921	59*	.846*	1928	54*	.709*
1915	4	.576	1922	35	.672*	1929	46*	.697*
1916	3	.419	1923	41*	.764*	1930	49*	.732*
1917	2	.472	1924	46*	.739*	1931	46*	.700*
1918	11*	.555*	1925	25	.543	1932	41	.661
1919	29*	.657*	1926	47*	.737*	1933	34	.582
1920	54*	.847*	1927	60*	.772*	1934	22	.537

of seeing him hit one ... than I do from hitting one myself."

— *Lou Gehrig*

Sultan of Swat, The Bambino

Also: Won 12 HR titles in a 14-year span and 12 slugging percentage titles in 13 seasons. Nobody has approached his .847 and .846 slugging percentages in 1920-21.

HALL OF FAME: 1936

4.02 HR-to-AB ratio: 1 every 11.8 at-bats

TSNdex power ranking: 288.1

Big Mac

Momentous clouts

It traveled an ordinary 370 feet to left field in Busch Stadium, but there was none bigger than No. 70, the second of two homers on the final day of the 1998 season off Montreal's Carl Pavano. No. 62 actually was his shortest of the '98 season, a 341-foot line drive just over the left-field wall at Busch Stadium off Chicago's Steve Trachsel. His longest in a memorable 1998 season was one 545-foot blast to center field in Busch Stadium on May 16.

2 MARK

6-5, 250 Career HRs: 522 Career slugging percentage: .587 HR-to-hit ratio: 1 to

"He's probably the strongest power hitter of all time."—*Padres manager Bruce Bochy*

"Never forget how amazing this man is. I keep searching for a way to describe it. It's even stranger than fiction, what this man has done and become."

—*Cardinals manager Tony La Russa*

Also: Only player to hit 50-plus homers in four consecutive seasons. Has averaged 64.3 homers over the last three seasons, and 61.25 over the last four. Hit a home run every 7.3 at-bats in 1998, better than Ruth's 9.0 in 1927 and Maris' 9.7 in 1961.

McGWIRE

2.87 HR-to-AB ratio: 1 every 10.8 at-bats

TSNdex power ranking: 227.9

3 JIMMIE FOXX

Momentous clouts

Take your pick from the man who also was known as "the righthanded Babe Ruth." He once cleared the double-decked stands at Comiskey Park, his titanic blast won the 1935 All-Star Game in Cleveland, and he broke a seat with a drive into the left field upper deck at Yankee Stadium.

5-11, 190 Career HRs: 534 Career slugging percentage: .609 HR-to-hit ratio: 1 to

1925	0	.778	1935	36*	.636*
1926	0	.438	1936	41	.631
1927	3	.515	1937	36	.538
1928	13	.548	1938	50	.704*
1929	33	.625	1939	35*	.694*
1930	37	.637	1940	36	.581
1931	30	.567	1941	19	.505
1932	58*	.749*	1942	8	.449
1933	48*	.703*	1944	0	.100
1934	44	.653	1945	7	.420

led league

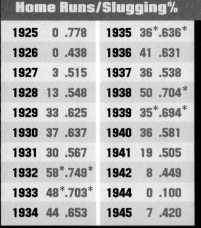

Double X

"It looked like a low line drive streaking over the infield, but it was still climbing when it clipped the very peak of the roofed upper deck in left and took off for the clouds. Three days later, a small boy in Bustleton, on the northeast fringe of town, found a baseball with snow on it."

—*Red Smith about a Shibe Park homer*

The Beast

4.96 HR-to-AB ratio: 1 every 15.2 at-bats

TSNdex power ranking: 242.5

17

> "The first time I saw Mantle, I knew how Paul Krichell felt when he first saw Lou Gehrig. He knew that as a scout, he'd never have another moment like it."
>
> —*Scout Tom Greenwade*

4 The Commerce Comet

MICKEY MANTLE

No explanation was needed for Casey Stengel and others who marveled at Mantle. The Mick was an artist with a bat.

HALL OF FAME: 1974

6-0, 201 Career HRs: 536 Career slugging percentage: .557 HR-to-hit ratio: 1 to

Home Runs/Slugging%
* led league

1951	13	.443	1960	40*	.558
1952	23	.530	1961	54	.687*
1953	21	.497	1962	30	.605*
1954	27	.525	1963	15	.622
1955	37*	.611*	1964	35	.591
1956	52*	.705*	1965	19	.452
1957	34	.665	1966	23	.538
1958	42*	.592	1967	22	.434
1959	31	.514	1968	18	.398

Also: Triple Crown winner in 1956 with .353 average, 52 homers and 130 RBIs.

> **"Mantle hits the longest ball in the game. He can belt it as far as Babe Ruth or Ted Williams, maybe farther."**
>
> —*Charlie Gehringer*

Momentous clouts

The term tape-measure home run came into vogue with his estimated 565-foot blast out of Griffith Stadium off Washington's Chuck Stobbs on April 17, 1953. Nobody ever has hit one out of Yankee Stadium, but he came close with a drive off the right-field facade, 390 feet away and 106 feet above the ground.

4.51 HR-to-AB ratio: 1 every 15.1 at-bats

TSNdex power ranking: 205.5

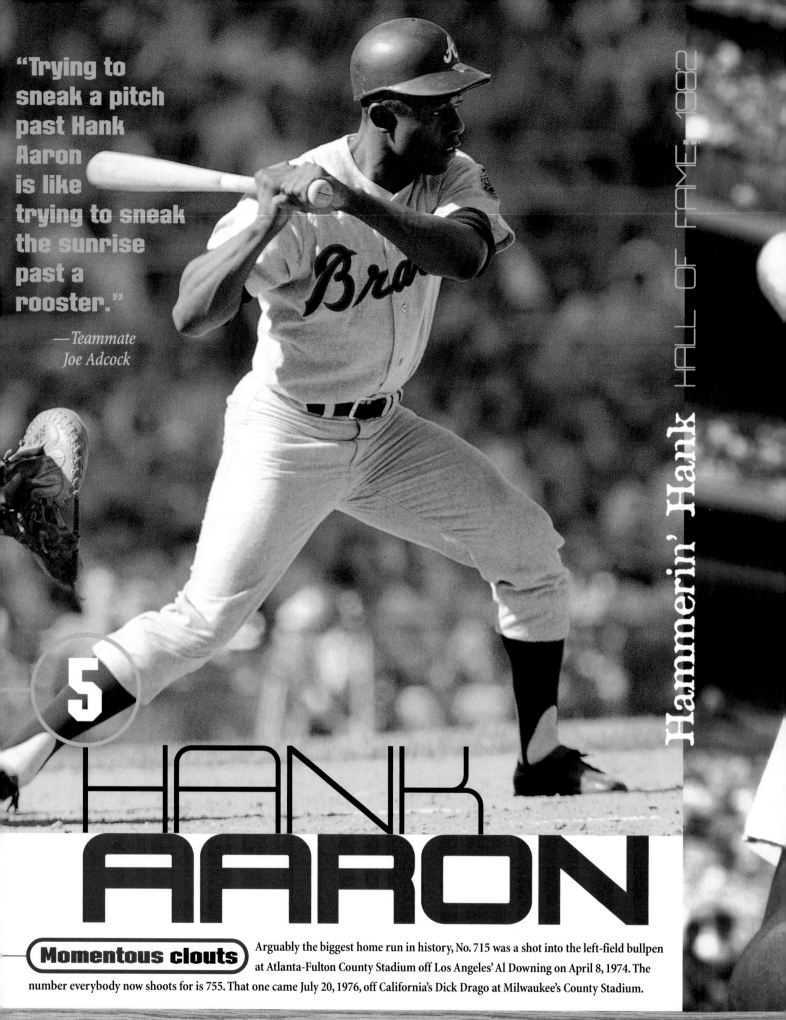

"Trying to sneak a pitch past Hank Aaron is like trying to sneak the sunrise past a rooster."

—*Teammate Joe Adcock*

5

HANK AARON

Momentous clouts Arguably the biggest home run in history, No. 715 was a shot into the left-field bullpen at Atlanta-Fulton County Stadium off Los Angeles' Al Downing on April 8, 1974. The number everybody now shoots for is 755. That one came July 20, 1976, off California's Dick Drago at Milwaukee's County Stadium.

6-0, 180 Career HRs: 755 Career slugging percentage: .555 HR-to-hit ratio: 1 to

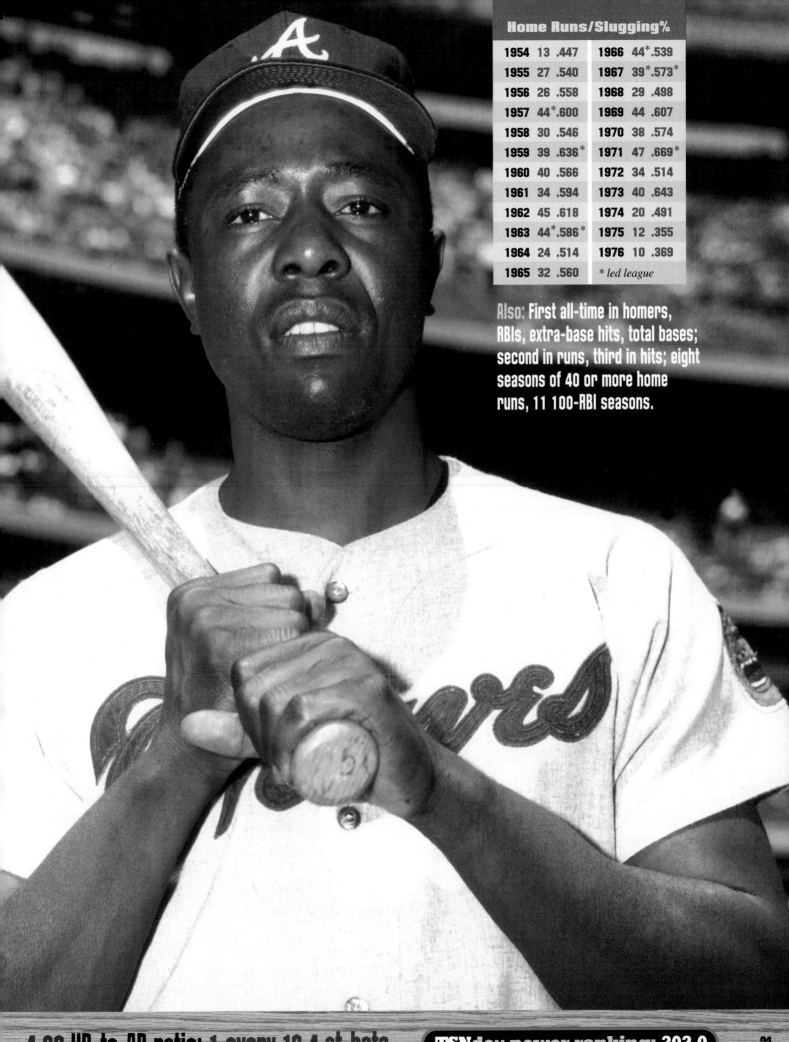

Home Runs/Slugging%

1954	13	.447	1966	44*	.539
1955	27	.540	1967	39*	.573*
1956	26	.558	1968	29	.498
1957	44*	.600	1969	44	.607
1958	30	.546	1970	38	.574
1959	39	.636*	1971	47	.669*
1960	40	.566	1972	34	.514
1961	34	.594	1973	40	.643
1962	45	.618	1974	20	.491
1963	44*	.586*	1975	12	.355
1964	24	.514	1976	10	.369
1965	32	.560			*led league*

Also: First all-time in homers, RBIs, extra-base hits, total bases; second in runs, third in hits; eight seasons of 40 or more home runs, 11 100-RBI seasons.

4.99 HR-to-AB ratio: 1 every 16.4 at-bats

TSNdex power ranking: 202.0

Year	HR	SLG
1951	20	.472
1952	4	.409
1954	41	.667*
1955	51*	.659*
1956	36	.557
1957	35	.626*
1958	29	.583
1959	34	.583
1960	29	.555
1961	40	.584
1962	49*	.615
1963	38	.582
1964	47*	.607*
1965	52*	.645*
1966	37	.556
1967	22	.453
1968	23	.488
1969	13	.437
1970	28	.506
1971	18	.482
1972	8	.402
1973	6	.344

led league

Also: Third all-time in homers and total bases, fourth in extra-base hits, led the National League in both homers and stolen bases four times, first player to hit 50 homers and steal 20 bases in the same season.

nentous clouts

There would be 659 more to follow, but No. 1 was memorable because it came off Warren Spahn, and sailed over the left-field roof at the Polo Grounds.

6

ILLEMAYS

5-11, 187 Career HRs: 660 Career slugging percentage: .557 HR-to-hit rat

"If somebody came up and hit .450, stole 100 bases and performed a miracle on the field every day, I'd still look you in the eye and say Willie was better."

—*Giants manager Leo Durocher*

The Say Hey Kid

Killer

6-0, 210 Career HRs: 573 Career slugging percentage: .509 HR-to-hit ratio: 1 to

	Home Runs/ Slugging%
1954	0 .385
1955	4 .363
1956	5 .394
1957	2 .548
1958	0 .194
1959	42* .516
1960	31 .534
1961	46 .606
1962	48* .545
1963	45* .555*
1964	49* .548
1965	25 .501
1966	39 .538
1967	44* .558
1968	17 .420
1969	49* .584
1970	41 .546
1971	28 .464
1972	26 .450
1973	5 .347
1974	13 .360
1975	14 .375

* led league

Also: No righthanded hitter in American League history has hit more home runs. Averaged 47 homers 1961-64, winning three of his six A.L. home run titles in that span.

7 HARMON KILLEBREW

Momentous clouts He was the first and one of only four righthanded hitters to clear the left-field roof at Tiger Stadium. The blast came on August 3, 1962, off Jim Bunning.

"Every time Harmon comes to the plate, he's dangerous. He is as good a clutch hitter as there is in the league. I have more respect for him than anyone."

—Boog Powell

3.64 HR-to-AB ratio: 1 every 14.2 at-bats   **TSNdex power ranking: 183.7**   25

"I'm the straw that

8

> "There isn't enough mustard in the world to cover that hot dog."
>
> —*Darold Knowles,*
> *Oakland teammate*

REGGIE JACKSON

6-0, 206 Career HRs: 563 Career slugging percentage: .490 HR-to-hit ratio: 1 to

Momentous clouts

In the 1971 All-Star Game, his towering blast off Dock Ellis hit a light tower atop the right-center-field roof of Detroit's Tiger Stadium. In Game 6 of the 1977 World Series, he hit homers off Burt Hooton, Elias Sosa and Charlie Hough to join Babe Ruth as the only players with three homers in a World Series game.

	Home Runs/ Slugging%	
1967	1	.305
1968	29	.452
1969	47	.608*
1970	23	.458
1971	32	.508
1972	25	.473
1973	32*	.531*
1974	29	.514
1975	36*	.511
1976	27	.502*
1977	32	.550
1978	27	.477
1979	29	.544
1980	41*	.597
1981	15	.428
1982	39*	.532
1983	14	.340
1984	25	.406
1985	27	.487
1986	18	.408
1987	15	.402

led league

HALL OF FAME: 1993

Mr. October

AB ratio: 1 every 17.5 at-bats   TSNdex power ranking: 172.2   27

Home Runs/Slugging%

Year	HR	SLG	Year	HR	SLG	Year	HR	SLG	Year	HR	SLG	Year	HR	SLG
1939	31	.609	1946	38	.667*	1950	28	.647	1954	29	.635	1958	26	.584
1940	23	.594	1947	32*	.634*	1951	30	.556*	1955	28	.703	1959	10	.419
1941	37*	.735*	1948	25	.615*	1952	1	.900	1956	24	.605	1960	29	.645
1942	36*	.648*	1949	43*	.650*	1953	13	.901	1957	38	.731*			*led league

Also: Won home run titles in 1941-42, 1947, 1949; RBI titles in 1942, 1947, 1949; and slugging percentage titles in 1941-42, 1946-49, 1951, 1957.

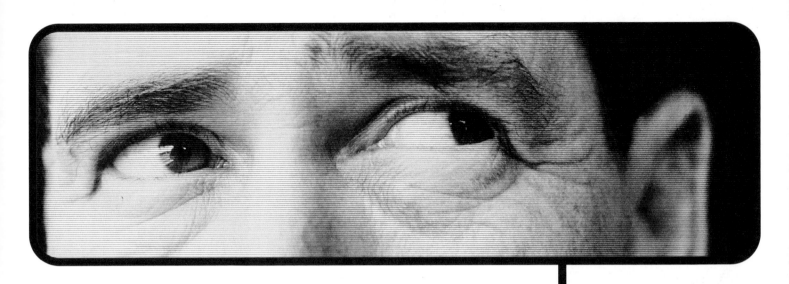

Momentous clouts

His three-run, ninth-inning blast off Claude Passeau in Detroit's Briggs Stadium won the 1941 All-Star Game. He also homered in his final big-league at-bat in 1960.

"Did they tell me how to pitch to Williams? Sure they did. ... They said he had no weaknesses, won't swing at a bad ball, had the best eyes in the business, and can kill you with one swing; he won't hit at anything bad, but don't give him anything good."

—Philadelphia A's pitcher Bobby Shantz

9

TED W

6-4, 198 Career HRs: 521 Career slugging percentage: .634 HR-to-hit ratio: 1 to

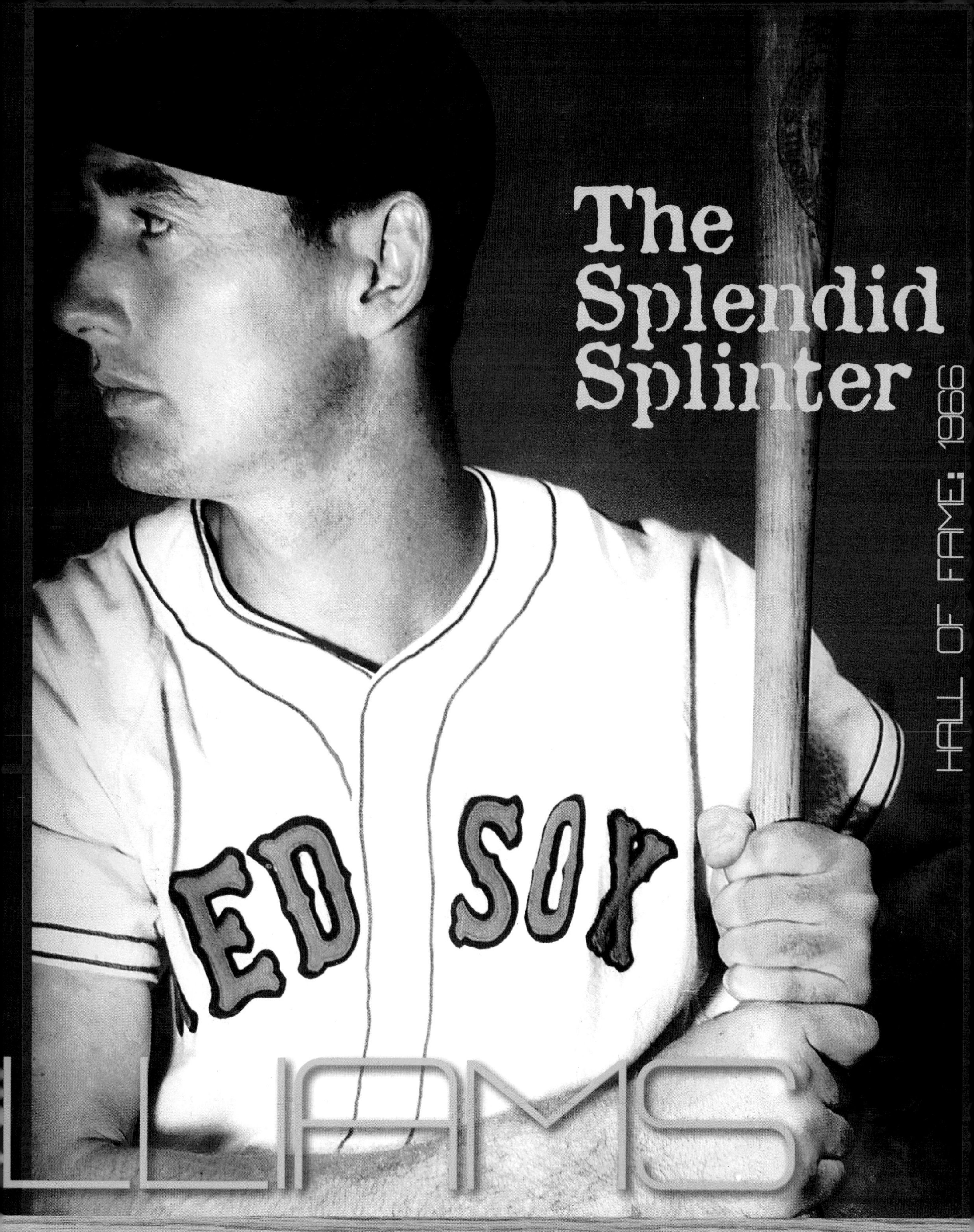

The Splendid Splinter

RED SOX

WILLIAMS

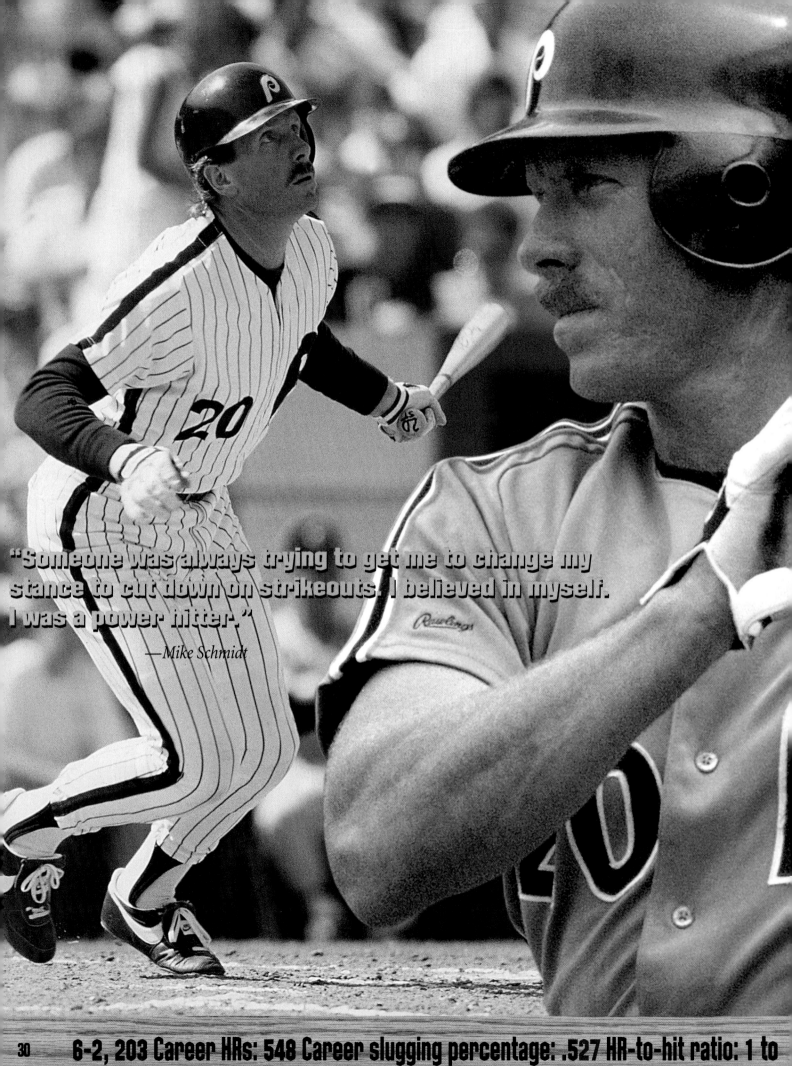

"Someone was always trying to get me to change my stance to cut down on strikeouts. I believed in myself. I was a power hitter."

—*Mike Schmidt*

6-2, 203 Career HRs: 548 Career slugging percentage: .527 HR-to-hit ratio: 1 to

MIKE ⑩ SCHMIDT
Smitty

Home Runs/Slugging%
* led league

1972	1	.294	**1981**	31*	.644*
1973	18	.373	**1982**	35	.547*
1974	36*	.546*	**1983**	40*	.524
1975	38*	.523	**1984**	36*	.536
1976	38*	.524	**1985**	33	.532
1977	38	.574	**1986**	37*	.547*
1978	21	.435	**1987**	35	.548
1979	45	.564	**1988**	12	.405
1980	48*	.624*	**1989**	6	.372

Also: Won eight National League HR titles, second-most in either league behind only Babe Ruth.

Momentous clouts

On July 17, 1976, Schmidt hit not one, but four home runs in consecutive at-bats at Wrigley Field in a wild 18-16 Phillies win. Two of the homers came off brothers Paul and Rick Reuschel. Wrigley Field again was the site on May 17, 1979, when Schmidt hit two homers, including the game-winner to cap an incredible 23-22 Phillies win in 10 innings. In 1974, he hit arguably the longest single in history, crushing a Claude Osteen fastball off a speaker dangling from the Astrodome roof, measured at 329 feet from home plate and 117 feet in the air.

HALL OF FAME: 1995

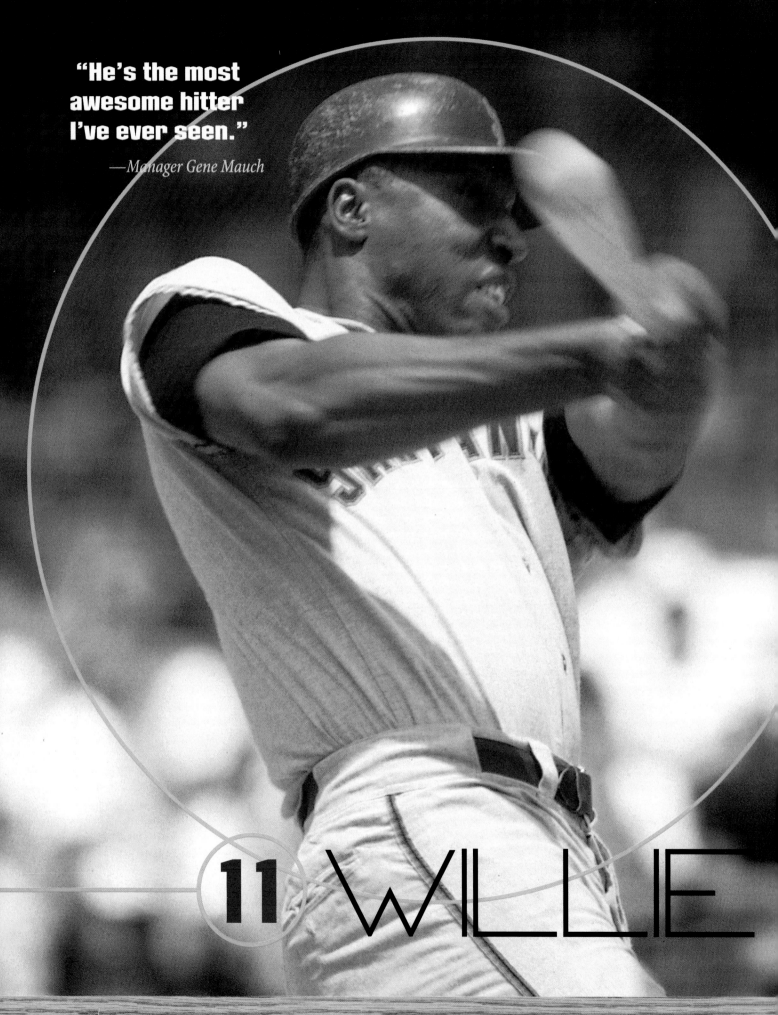

"He's the most awesome hitter I've ever seen."

—*Manager Gene Mauch*

11 WILLIE

6-4, 225 Career HRs: 521 Career slugging percentage: .515 HR-to-hit ratio: 1 to

1959	13	.656	1963	44*	.566	1967	31	.535	1971	18	.480	1975	23	.460	1979	15	.402
1960	13	.469	1964	18	.412	1968	36*	.545*	1972	14	.403	1976	7	.336	1980	16	.301
1961	18	.491	1965	39	.539	1969	45*	.656*	1973	29	.546	1977	28	.500			
1962	20	.590	1966	36	.586	1970	39	.612*	1974	22	.506	1978	12	.396	*led league		

Also: Averaged 40 homers, 119 RBIs with two N.L. home run titles and three slugging percentage titles in 1968-70.

Stretch

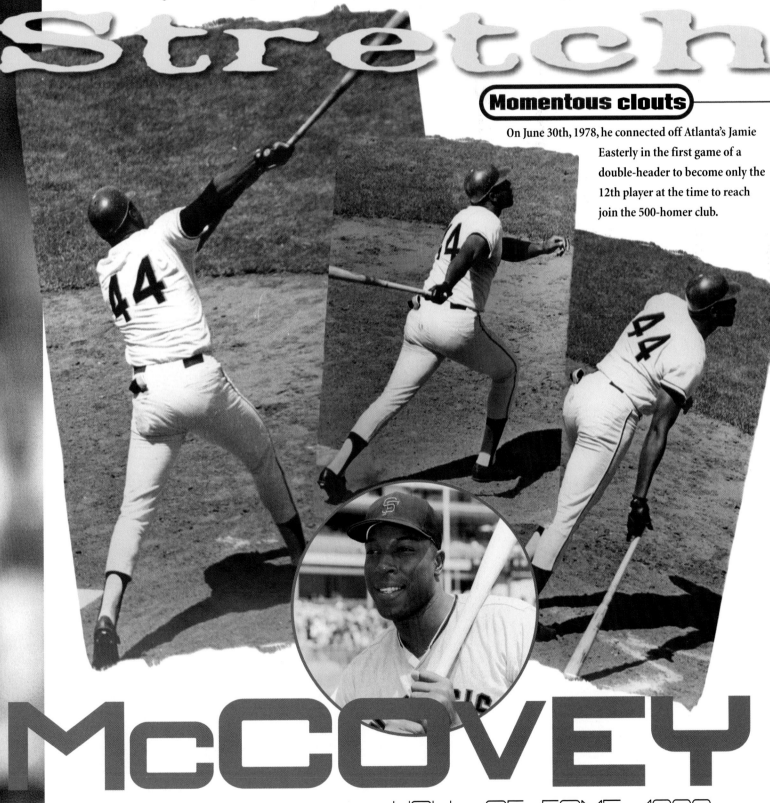

Momentous clouts

On June 30th, 1978, he connected off Atlanta's Jamie Easterly in the first game of a double-header to become only the 12th player at the time to reach join the 500-homer club.

McCOVEY

HALL OF FAME: 1986

4.24 HR-to-AB ratio: 1 every 15.7 at-bats   **TSNdex power ranking: 186.5**   33

Home Runs/ Slugging% *led league		
1989	16	.420
1990	22	.481
1991	22	.527
1992	27	.535
1993	45	.617
1994	40*	.674
1995	17	.481
1996	49	.628
1997	56*	.646*
1998	56*	.611
1999	48*	.576

Also: Averaged 52 homers and 142 RBIs in 1996-99.

HEN

12

Momentous clouts

He belted three homers on April 25, 1997, against Toronto, the third being No. 250 in his career, and making him the fourth-youngest to reach that plateau. He reached the upper deck in center field in Toronto's Skydome on April 12, 1996.

Junior

6-3, 205 Career HRs: 398 Career slugging percentage: .569 HR-to-hit ratio: 1 to

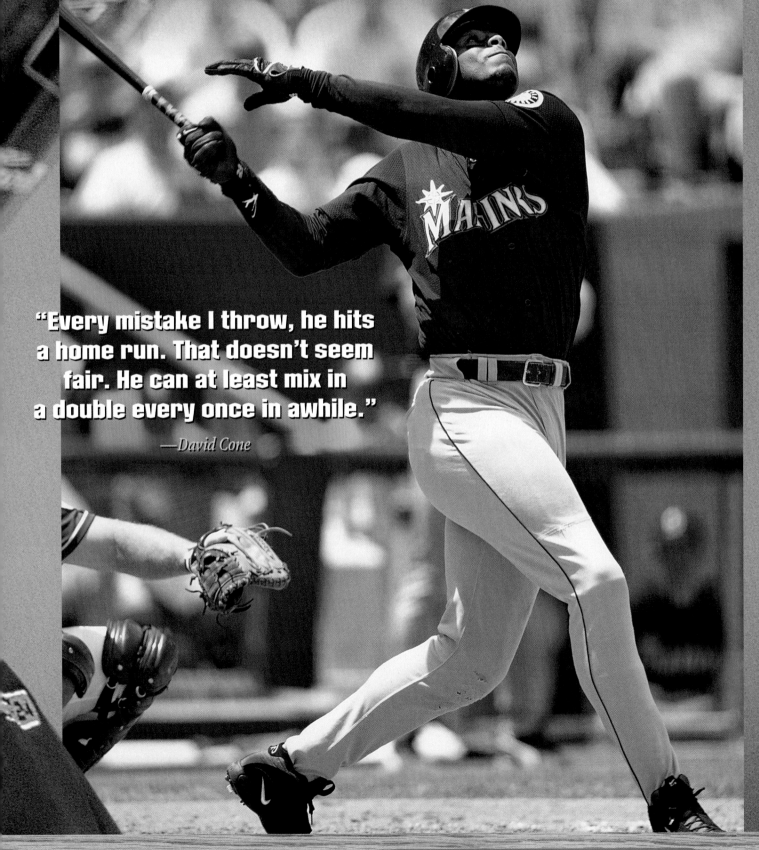

GRIFFEY JR.

"Every mistake I throw, he hits a home run. That doesn't seem fair. He can at least mix in a double every once in awhile."

—David Cone

> "Lou Gehrig was a man who came through in the clutch above all others."
> —*Joe McCarthy*

The Iron Horse

Momentous clouts

Four of his 493 regular-season homers came in the same game, on June 3, 1932, in Shibe Park. Nobody has hit more grand slams—23—including four in 1934. His 10th and final World Series home run came on October 9, 1937 off Carl Hubbell.

13

LOU GEH

HALL OF FAME: 1939

6-1, 200 Career HRs: 493 Career slugging percentage: .632 HR-to-hit ratio: 1 to

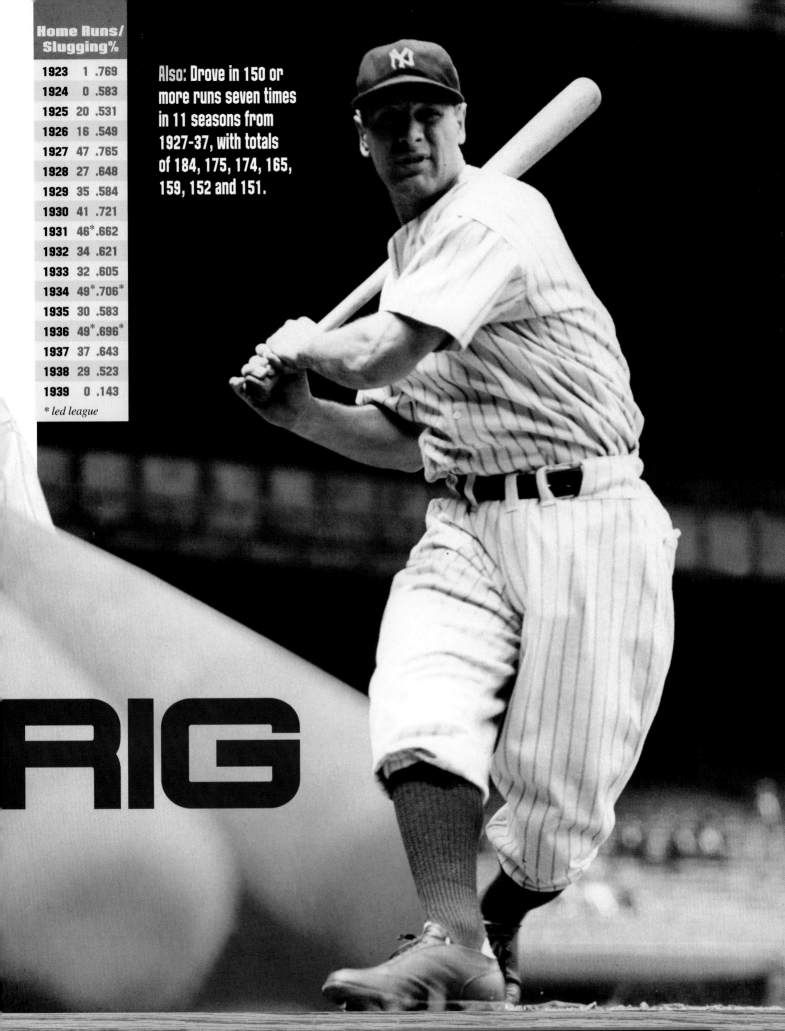

Home Runs/Slugging%		
1923	1	.769
1924	0	.583
1925	20	.531
1926	16	.549
1927	47	.765
1928	27	.648
1929	35	.584
1930	41	.721
1931	46*	.662
1932	34	.621
1933	32	.605
1934	49*	.706*
1935	30	.583
1936	49*	.696*
1937	37	.643
1938	29	.523
1939	0	.143

led league

Also: Drove in 150 or more runs seven times in 11 seasons from 1927-37, with totals of 184, 175, 174, 165, 159, 152 and 151.

RIG

5.51 HR-to-AB ratio: 1 every 16.2 at-bats

TSNdex power ranking: 259.6

14

RA

6-2, 195 Career HRs: 369 Career slugging percentage: .548 HR-to-hit ratio: 1 to

"singles hitters drive Fords."

—*Pittsburgh teammate Fritz Ostermueller on Kiner's $90,000 salary in 1951*

	Home Runs/ Slugging%	
1946	23*	.430
1947	51*	.639*
1948	40*	.533
1949	54*	.658*
1950	47*	.590
1951	42*	.627*
1952	37*	.500
1953	35	.512
1954	22	.487
1955	18	.452

* led league

Also:
Won N.L. home run titles seven consecutive years, 1946-52, averaging 42 per season.

RALPH KINER

Momentous clouts

He set a major-league record with eight homers in four games September 10-12 en route to 51 homers in 1947. With 54 homers in 1949—including 16 in September — he was the first to reach 50 since Hank Greenberg 11 years earlier.

3.93 HR-to-AB ratio: 1 every 14.1 at-bats   TSNdex power ranking: 205.4

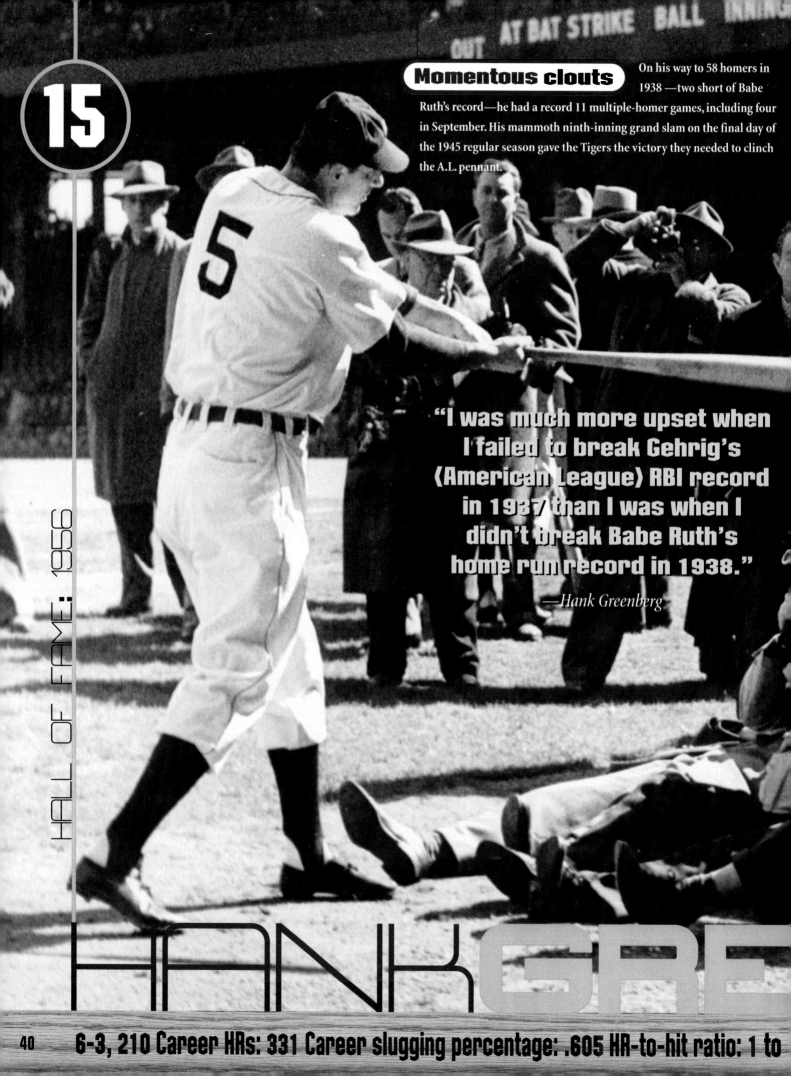

HALL OF FAME: 1956

Momentous clouts

On his way to 58 homers in 1938 —two short of Babe Ruth's record—he had a record 11 multiple-homer games, including four in September. His mammoth ninth-inning grand slam on the final day of the 1945 regular season gave the Tigers the victory they needed to clinch the A.L. pennant.

"I was much more upset when I failed to break Gehrig's (American League) RBI record in 1937 than I was when I didn't break Babe Ruth's home run record in 1938."

—*Hank Greenberg*

HANK GRE

6-3, 210 Career HRs: 331 Career slugging percentage: .605 HR-to-hit ratio: 1 to

Hammerin' Hank

Home Runs/Slugging%

1933	12	.468	1939	33	.622
1934	26	.600	1940	41*	.670*
1935	36*	.628	1941	2	.463
1936	1	.630	1945	13	.544
1937	40	.668	1946	44	.604
1938	58*	.683	1947	25	.478

Also: Had seven consecutive seasons with a slugging percentage above .600; drove in 1,276 runs in 1,394 games.

GREENBERG

4.9 HR-to-AB ratio: 1 every 15.7 at-bats

TSNdex power ranking: 244.4

FRANK

Home Runs/Slugging%
led league

1956	38	.558	1963	21	.442	1970	25	.520
1957	29	.529	1964	29	.548	1971	28	.510
1958	31	.504	1965	33	.540	1972	19	.442
1959	36	.583	1966	49*	.637*	1973	30	.489
1960	31	.595*	1967	30	.576	1974	22	.453
1961	37	.611*	1968	15	.444	1975	9	.508
1962	39	.624*	1969	32	.540	1976	3	.358

Also: Won three consecutive slugging percentage titles 1960-62, and the Triple Crown plus the slugging percentage title in 1966.

"Pitchers did me a favor when they knocked me down.

It made me more determined.
I wouldn't let that pitcher get me out.
They say you can't hit if you're on your back.
But I didn't hit on my back.
I got up."

—*Frank Robinson*

6-1, 195 Career HRs: 586 Career slugging percentage: .537 HR-to-hit ratio: 1 to

OBINSON (16)

Momentous clouts

All he did in his first at-bat as manager/cleanup hitter for the 1975 Indians was belt a first-inning home run—his record eighth on Opening Day.

HALL OF FAME: 1982

5.02 HR-to-AB ratio: 1 every 17.07 at-bats   **TSN**dex power ranking: 193.9   43

"I've only known three or four perfect swings in my time. This lad has one of them."

—*Ty Cobb*

Momentous clouts

In his rookie season of 1952, he hit three on September 27 in Ebbets Field. He won game 4 of the 1957 World Series with a 10th-inning homer off Bob Grim. On June 8, 1961, he was the first of four Milwaukee Braves to hit consecutive homers, followed by Hank Aaron, Joe Adcock and Frank Thomas.

6-1, 195 Career HRs: 512 Career slugging percentage: .509 HR-to-hit ratio: 1 to

"He swings the bat faster than anyone I ever saw. You think you've got a called strike past him, and he hits it out of the catcher's glove."

—*Carl Erskine*

Mathews and Hank Aaron formed a powerful combination for the Braves in the 1950s and '60s.

17

Also: Hit 40 or more home runs four times 1953-59

	Home Runs/Slugging%				
1952	25 .447	1958	31 .458	1964	23 .412
1953	47*.627	1959	46*.593	1965	32 .469
1954	40 .603	1960	39 .551	1966	16 .420
1955	41 .601	1961	32 .535	1967	16 .392
1956	37 .518	1962	29 .496	1968	3 .397
1957	32 .540	1963	23 .453	*led league	

EDDIE MATHEWS

4.52 HR-to-AB ratio: 1 every 16.7 at-bats

TSNdex power ranking: 183.7

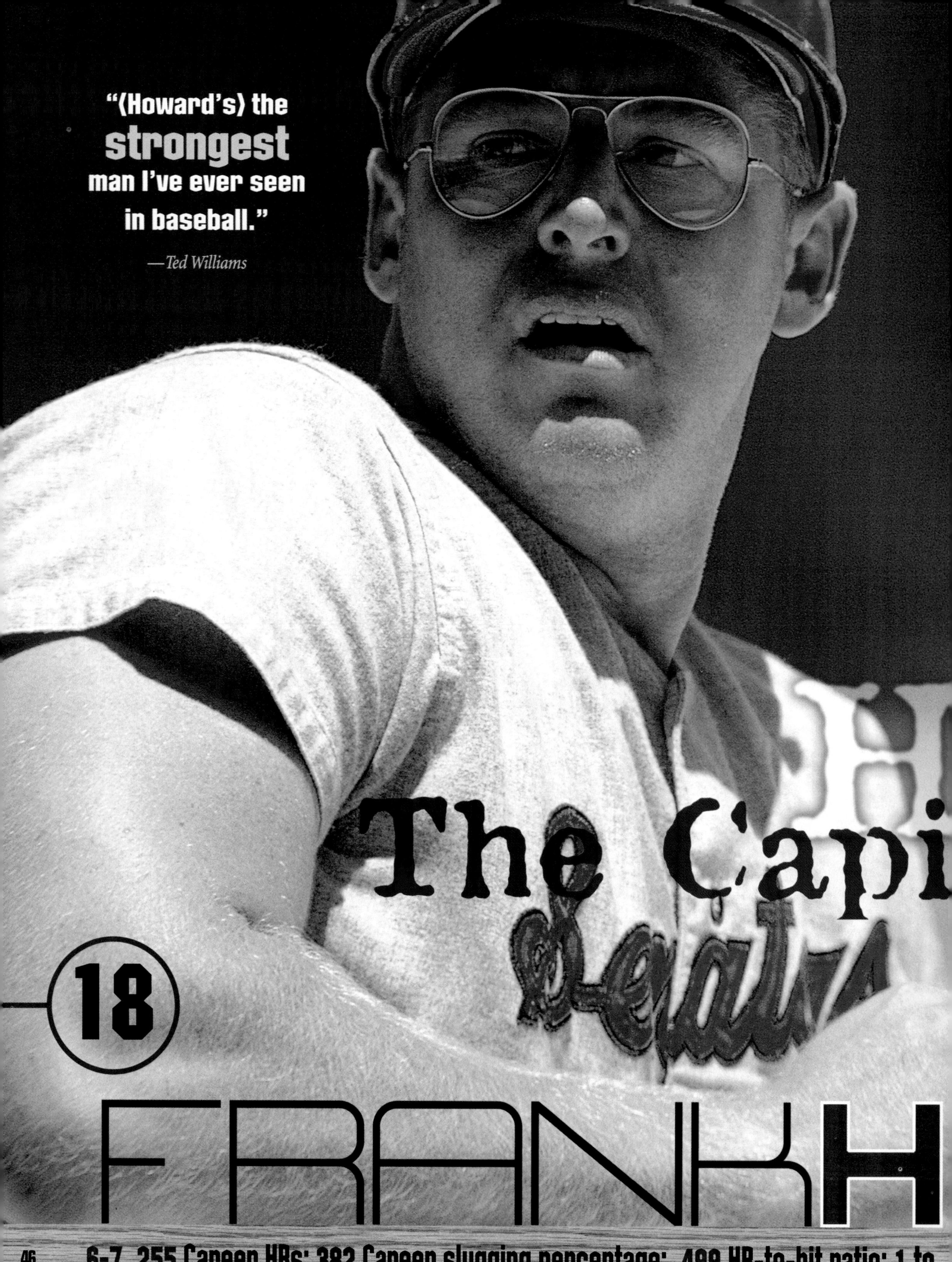

"(Howard's) the **strongest** man I've ever seen in baseball."

—*Ted Williams*

The Capi

18

FRANK H

6-7, 255 Career HRs: 382 Career slugging percentage: .499 HR-to-hit ratio: 1 to

Home Runs/Slugging%		* led league										
1958	1	.379	1960	23	.464	1962	31	.560	1964	24	.432	1966	18	.442	1968	44*	.552*	1970	44*	.546	1972	10	.369
1959	1	.381	1961	15	.517	1963	28	.518	1965	21	.477	1967	36	.511	1969	48	.574	1971	26	.474	1973	12	.463

Also: Hit a major-league leading 172 homers and won two home run titles 1967-70.

Momentous clouts

Nobody hit more homers—10—in fewer at-bats—20—a six-game rampage in May, 1968.

tol Punisher

OWARD

4.6 HR-to-AB ratio: 1 every 17.0 at-bats

TSNdex power ranking: 173.4

47

19 JOSE
CANSECO

6-4, 240 Career HRs: 431 Career slugging percentage: .520 HR-to-hit ratio: 1 to

1985	5 .490	1987	31 .470	1989	17 .542	1991	44*.556	1993	10 .455	1995	24 .556	1997	23 .461	1999	34 .563
1986	33 .457	1988	42*.569*	1990	37 .543	1992	26 .456	1994	31 .552	1996	28 .589	1998	46 .518		*led league

Also: Two home-run titles, one RBI title, three 40-plus-homer seasons. First 40-40 player in history.

Momentous clouts

His 40th homer of 1988 made him the first player to hit 40 homers and steal 40 bases in the same season. He started the 1988 World Series with a bang—a Game 1 grand slam off Tim Belcher (only to have it overshadowed later that game by a guy named Kirk Gibson). He became the first player to reach the fifth deck in Toronto's Skydome, and did it in Game 4 of the 1989 American League Championship Series.

"He's the most devastating offensive machine in baseball history. I've seen him hit home runs to right field that you would have thought were hit by Willie Stargell or Mickey Mantle."

—*Dave Parker*

Brother

4.01 HR-to-AB ratio: 1 every 15.0 at-bats

TSNdex power ranking: 188.3

"I can't name a player who has exerted as strong an influence upon so many games as Mel."
—*Pie Traynor*

Momentous clouts

With a swing tailored to the Polo Grounds' short right-field porch, he hit 323 of his 511 homers there.

Master Melvin

5-9, 170 Career HRs: 511 Career slugging percentage: .533 HR-to-hit ratio: 1 to

Home Runs/ Slugging%		
1926	0	.417
1927	1	.380
1928	18	.524
1929	42	.635
1930	25	.578
1931	29	.545
1932	38*	.601
1933	23	.467
1934	35*	.591
1935	31	.555
1936	33*	.588*
1937	31*	.523
1938	36*	.583
1939	27	.581
1940	19	.457
1941	27	.495
1942	30*	.497
1943	18	.418
1944	26	.544
1945	21	.499
1946	1	.132

led league

Also: Won five N.L. home run titles in seven years, 1932-38, and was the first National Leaguer to hit 500 homers.

20

MEL OTT

5.6 HR-to-AB ratio: 1 every 18.5 at-bats

TSNdex power ranking: 191.2

SAMMY

21

"My feeling that what Sammy and I have done, nobody should be disappointed. We're two guys who have done something that's never been done in the history of the game."

—*Mark McGwire*

6-0, 210 Career HRs: 336 Career slugging percentage: .510 HR-to-hit ratio: 1 to

SOSA

Home Runs/Slugging%			
1989	4 .366	1995	36 .500
1990	15 .404	1996	40 .564
1991	10 .335	1997	36 .480
1992	8 .393	1998	66 .647
1993	33 .485	1999	63 .635
1994	25 .545		

Also: Only he and McGwire have hit 60 homers in more than one season.

Momentous clouts

He tied and passed Roger Maris on the same day—September 12, 1998—with a pair of 480-foot homers in an 11-10 win at Milwaukee. Nobody in history reached 66 homers faster—but not by much. No. 66 came on September 25, 1998, in a Cubs loss, and only temporarily gave him the home run lead, as Mark McGwire struck again 58 minutes later in St. Louis. No. 63 that year was a game-winning grand slam at San Diego on September 15.

Slammin' Sammy

4.2 HR-to-AB ratio: 1 every 15.7 at-bats

TSNdex power ranking: 183.7

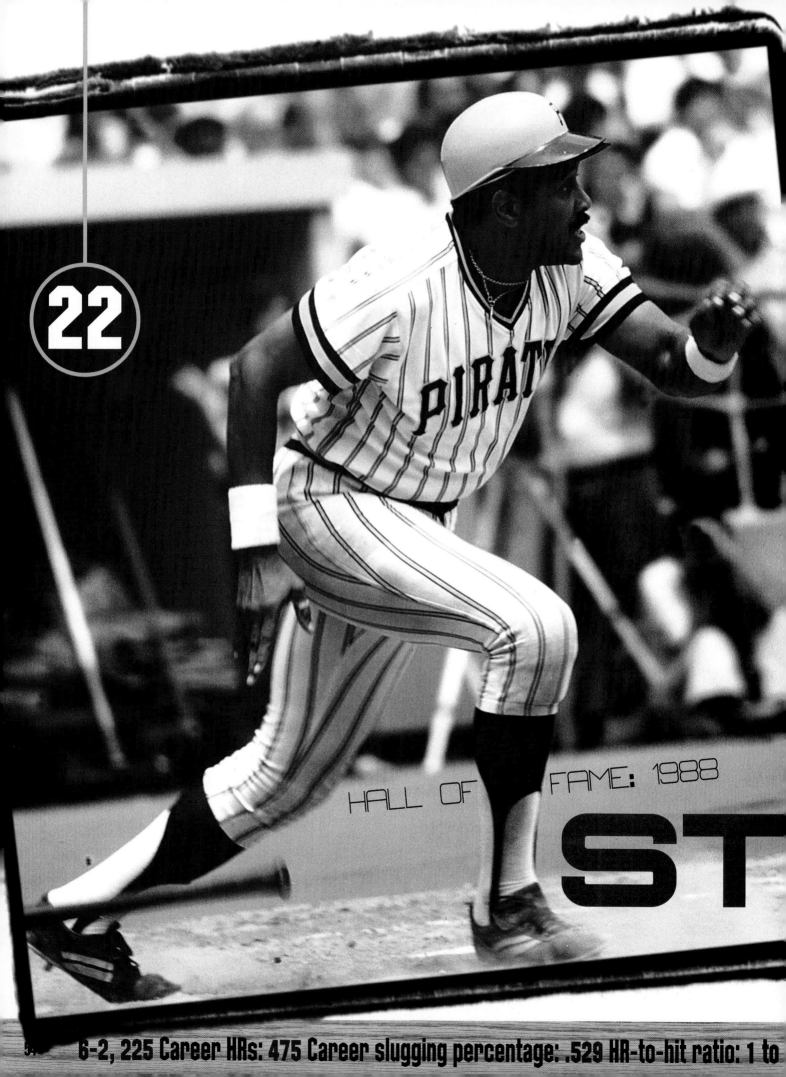

22

HALL OF FAME: 1988

ST

6-2, 225 Career HRs: 475 Career slugging percentage: .529 HR-to-hit ratio: 1 to

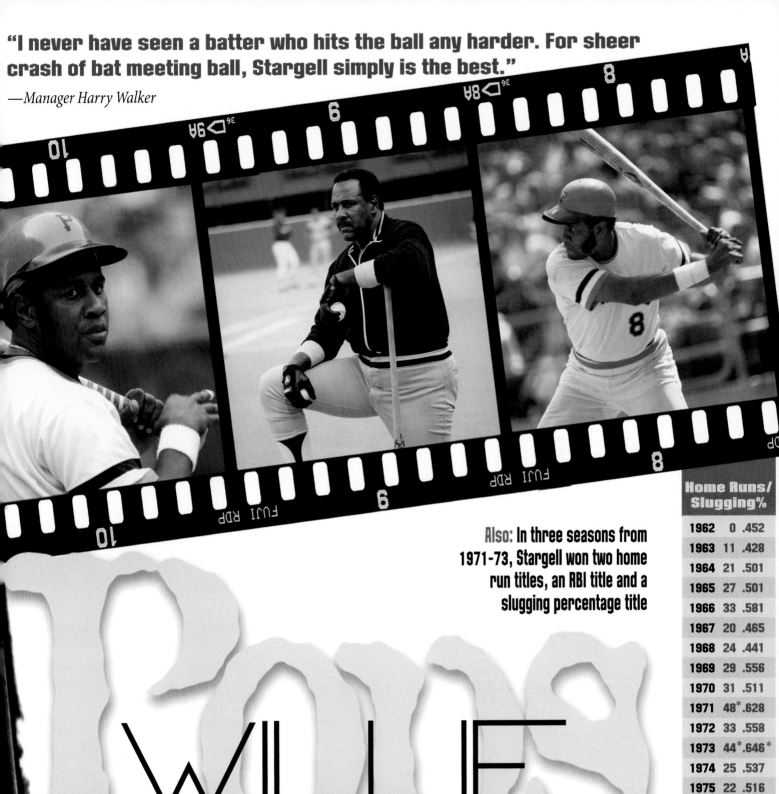

> "I never have seen a batter who hits the ball any harder. For sheer crash of bat meeting ball, Stargell simply is the best."
> —*Manager Harry Walker*

Also: In three seasons from 1971-73, Stargell won two home run titles, an RBI title and a slugging percentage title

Bang
WILLIE
ARGELL

	Home Runs/ Slugging%
1962	0 .452
1963	11 .428
1964	21 .501
1965	27 .501
1966	33 .581
1967	20 .465
1968	24 .441
1969	29 .556
1970	31 .511
1971	48*.628
1972	33 .558
1973	44*.646*
1974	25 .537
1975	22 .516
1976	20 .458
1977	13 .548
1978	28 .567
1979	32 .552
1980	11 .485
1981	0 .350
1982	3 .411

* *led league*

Momentous clouts

He hit no fewer than seven over the right field roof at Forbes Field, four into the upper deck at Three Rivers Stadium, the only two balls entirely out of Dodger Stadium, and one in Montreal's Olympic Stadium measured at 535 feet.

4.7 HR-to-AB ratio: 1 every 16.7 at-bats   **TSNdex power ranking: 194.1**   55

ROCKY COLAVITO (23)

The Rock

"Fundamentally he doesn't have a weakness, except for his own **intensity.** He can hit any kind of pitch to any part of the field."

—*Joe Gordon in 1959*

6-3, 190 Career HRs: 374 Career slugging percentage: .489 HR-to-hit ratio: 1 to

Home Runs/Slugging%
led league

Year	HR	SLG%	Year	HR	SLG%
1955	0	.667	1962	37	.514
1956	21	.531	1963	22	.437
1957	25	.471	1964	34	.507
1958	41	.620*	1965	26	.468
1959	42*	.512	1966	30	.432
1960	35	.474	1967	8	.333
1961	45	.580	1968	8	.382

Also: He hit 83 homers and won one home-run title and one slugging percentage title in 1958-59, and averaged 40 homers per season 1958-62.

Momentous clouts

In a 42-homer season in 1959, he hit home runs in four consecutive at-bats on June 10 in Baltimore.

"I feel in my heart that no matter how I'm hitting, I'm going to get a hit whenever I go up to the plate."

—*Rocky Colavito*

4.6 HR-to-AB ratio: 1 every 17.4 at-bats   TSNdex power ranking: 168.6

HALL OF FAME: 1955

Momentous clouts

To break Wee Willie Keeler's old major-league mark of hitting in 44 consecutive games, he slugged a home run off Dick Newsome. The Streak, of course, reached 56 games, during which he hit 15 homers. He also slugged a then-major-league record 15 homers in July en route to 46 in 1937.

"As far as I'm concerned, Joe DiMaggio was

6-2, 193 Career HRs: 361 Career slugging percentage: .579 HR-to-hit ratio: 1 to

DiMAGGIO
Yankee Clipper

Also: Won home run titles 11 years apart, 1937 and 1948, and slugging percentage titles 13 years apart, 1937 and 1950. Struck out only 369 times, eight more than his home run total.

"...robably the greatest all-around baseball player who ever lived."

—Mickey Mantle

Stan The Man

"I throw him four wide ones

25 STAN
MU

6-0, 180 Career HRs: 475 Career slugging percentage: .559 HR-to-hit ratio: 1 to

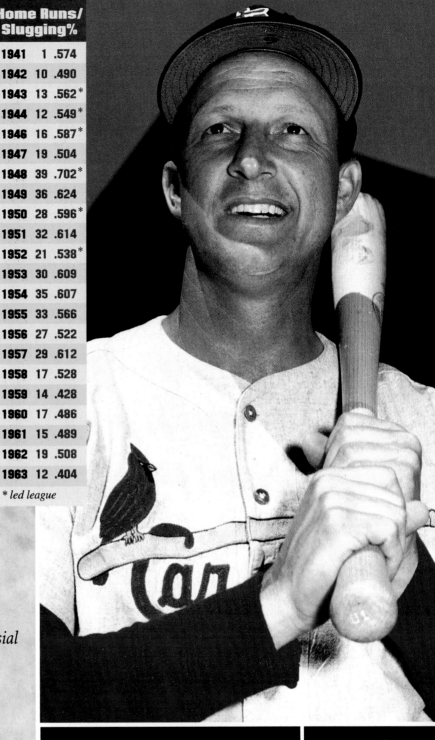

Momentous clouts

He set a major-league record on May 2, 1954, by hitting five home runs in a doubleheader. His record six homers in All-Star Game competition included a game-winner in the 12th inning of the 1955 game.

Home Runs/ Slugging%		
1941	1	.574
1942	10	.490
1943	13	.562*
1944	12	.549*
1946	16	.587*
1947	19	.504
1948	39	.702*
1949	36	.624
1950	28	.596*
1951	32	.614
1952	21	.538*
1953	30	.609
1954	35	.607
1955	33	.566
1956	27	.522
1957	29	.612
1958	17	.528
1959	14	.428
1960	17	.486
1961	15	.489
1962	19	.508
1963	12	.404

* led league

Also: Won six batting titles, six slugging percentage titles and one RBI title 1943-52. Missed the Triple Crown in 1948 by just one home run.

and then I try to pick him off."

— Preacher Roe, giving advice on how to pitch to Musial

SIAL

HALL OF FAME: 1969

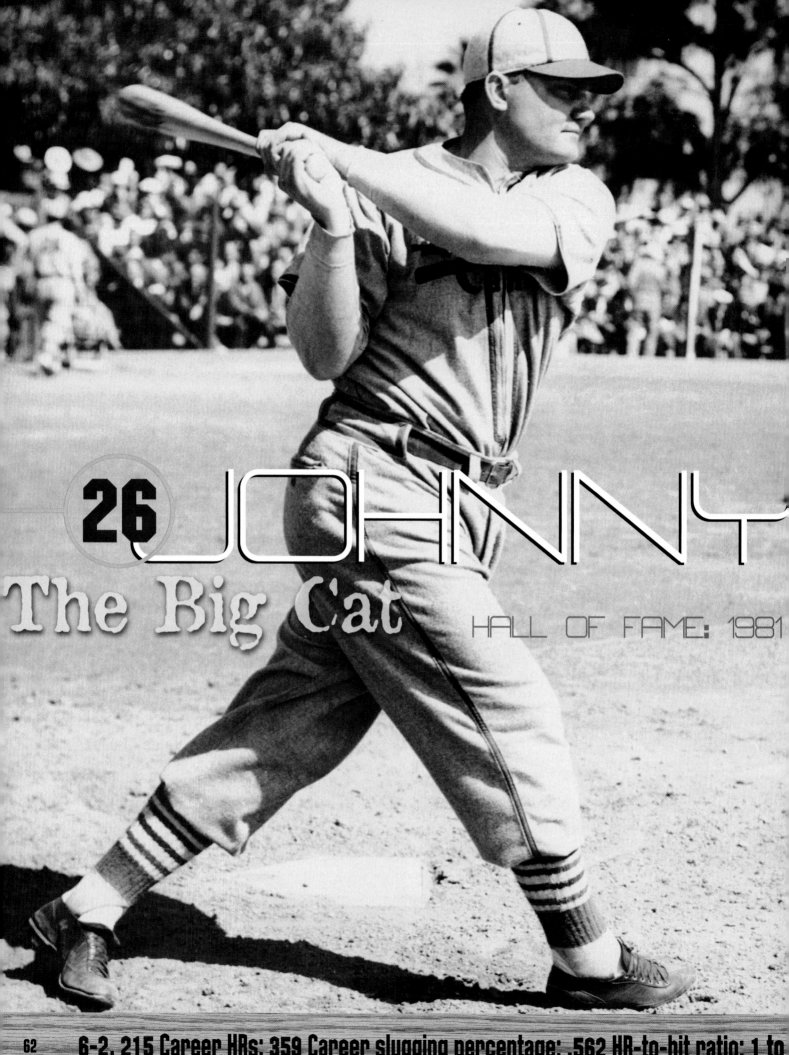

26 JOHNNY

The Big Cat

HALL OF FAME: 1981

6-2, 215 Career HRs: 359 Career slugging percentage: .562 HR-to-hit ratio: 1 to

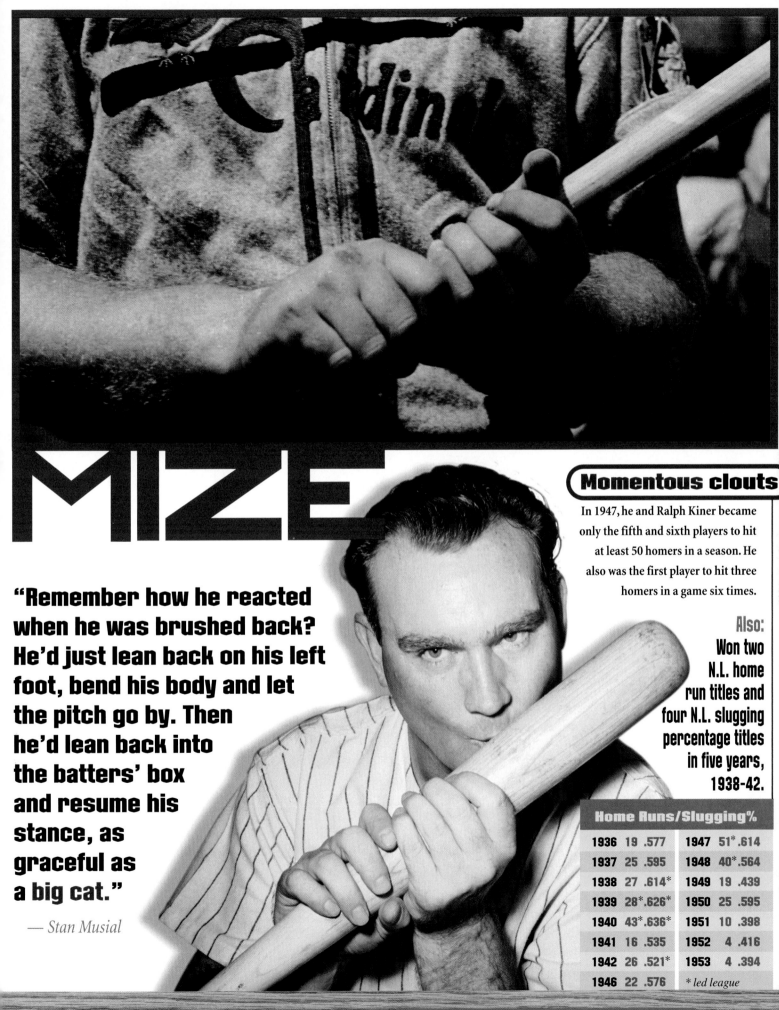

MIZE

> "Remember how he reacted when he was brushed back? He'd just lean back on his left foot, bend his body and let the pitch go by. Then he'd lean back into the batters' box and resume his stance, as graceful as a big cat."
>
> — *Stan Musial*

Home Runs/Slugging%			
1936	19 .577	1947	51*.614
1937	25 .595	1948	40*.564
1938	27 .614*	1949	19 .439
1939	28*.626*	1950	25 .595
1940	43*.636*	1951	10 .398
1941	16 .535	1952	4 .416
1942	26 .521*	1953	4 .394
1946	22 .576	*led league	

5.6 HR-to-AB ratio: 1 every 17.9 at-bats   TSNdex power ranking: 213.1

27

the Duke of Flatbush

"In the split second from the time the ball leaves the pitcher's hand until it reaches the plate, you have to think about your stride, your hip action, your wrist action, determine how much, if any, the ball is going to break and then decide whether to swing at it." —*Duke Snider*

6-0, 190 Career HRs: 407 Career slugging percentage: .540 HR-to-hit ratio: 1 to

DUKE SNIDER

Home Runs/Slugging%			* led league					
1947	0	.301	1953	42	.627*	1959	23	.535
1948	5	.450	1954	40	.647	1960	14	.519
1949	23	.493	1955	42	.628	1961	16	.562
1950	31	.553	1956	43*	.598*	1962	5	.481
1951	29	.483	1957	40	.587	1963	14	.401
1952	21	.494	1958	15	.505	1964	4	.323

Also: Hit 40 or more homers five consecutive years 1953-57, with three runs scored titles, two slugging percentage titles and one RBI title.

Silver Fox

Momentous clouts

The postseason homer was his specialty, as he is the only player to hit four homers in two different World Series, 1952 and 1955, and has the National League World Series home run and RBI marks with 11 and 26.

5.2 HR-to-AB ratio: 1 every 17.6 at-bats

TSNdex power ranking: 200.7

Momentous clouts He became the sixth-fastest player to reach the 250-homer mark with a blast in Comiskey Park on May 24th, 1997, off Milwaukee's Jeff D'Amico, and set a major-league record with 31 homers after August 1 in 1995.

(28) ALBERT

6-2, 225 Career HRs: 358 Career slugging percentage: .573 HR-to-hit ratio: 1 to

Home Runs/Slugging%			
1989	7 .394	1995	50*.690*
1990	1 .304	1996	48 .623
1991	28 .540	1997	30 .491
1992	34 .477	1998	49 .655*
1993	38 .552	1999	37 .573
1994	36 .714	* led league	

baseball history."

—Indians General Manager John Hart

Also: Won one home run title, three RBI titles and two slugging percentage titles from 1993-98. Is the only player in history to hit 50 homers and 50 doubles in the same season.

BELLE

4.4 HR-to-AB ratio: 1 every 14.8 at-bats

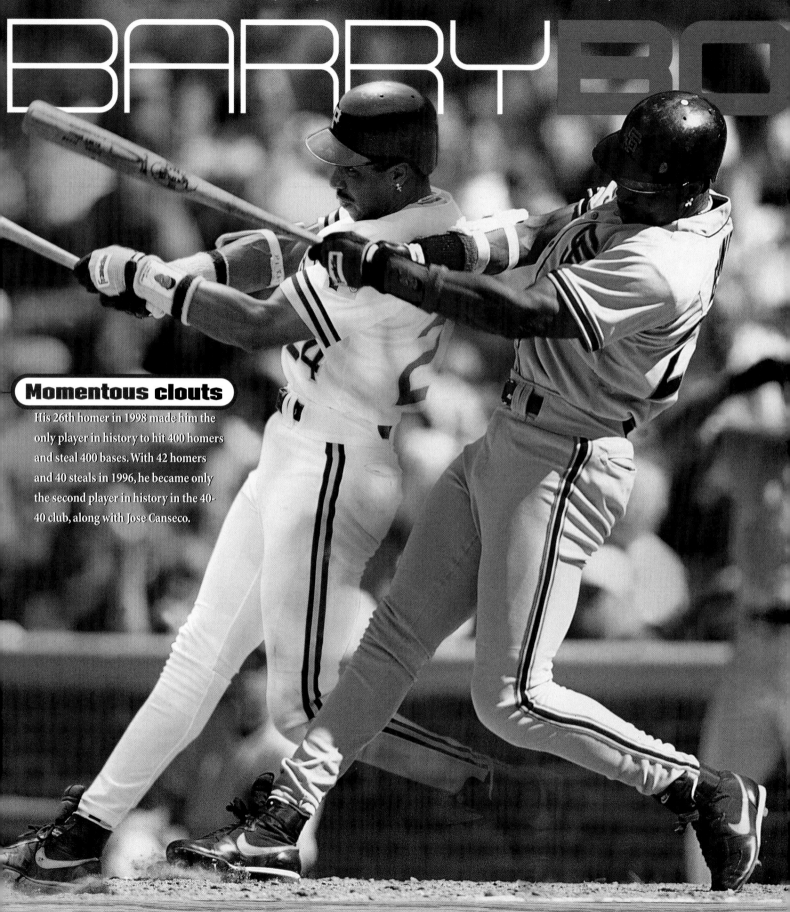

Home Runs/Slugging%

| 1986 | 16 .416 | 1988 | 24 .491 | 1990 | 33 .565 | 1992 | 34 .624 | 1994 | 37 .647 | 1996 | 42 .615 | 1998 | 37 .609 |
| 1987 | 25 .492 | 1989 | 19 .426 | 1991 | 25 .514 | 1993 | 46 .677 | 1995 | 33 .577 | 1997 | 40 .585 | 1999 | 34 .617 |

Also: He and father Bobby own the major-league records for father-son combinations in homers, RBI and stolen bases.

BARRY 30

Momentous clouts

His 26th homer in 1998 made him the only player in history to hit 400 homers and steal 400 bases. With 42 homers and 40 steals in 1996, he became only the second player in history in the 40-40 club, along with Jose Canseco.

6-1, 190 Career HRs: 445 Career slugging percentage: .559 HR-to-hit ratio: 1 to

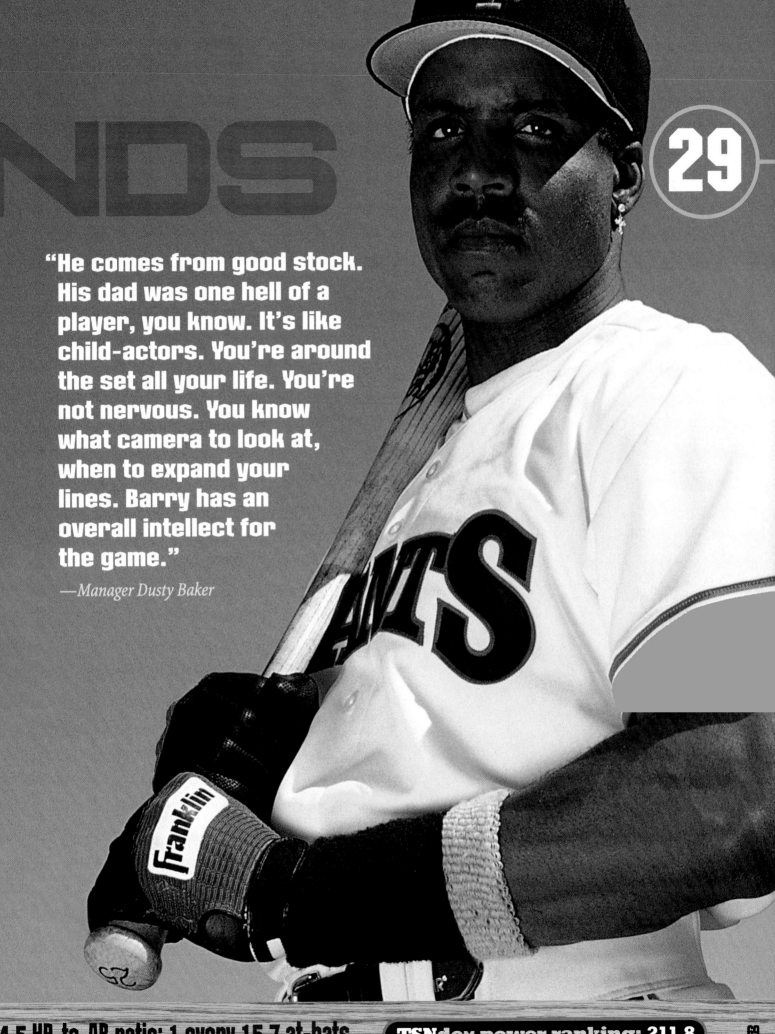

"He comes from good stock. His dad was one hell of a player, you know. It's like child-actors. You're around the set all your life. You're not nervous. You know what camera to look at, when to expand your lines. Barry has an overall intellect for the game."

—*Manager Dusty Baker*

JUAN GON

30

6-3, 220 Career HRs: 340 Career slugging percentage: .572 HR-to-hit ratio: 1 to

...ZALEZ

Home Runs/Slugging%

1989	1 .250	1993	46*.632*	1997	42 .589
1990	4 .522	1994	19 .472	1998	45 .630
1991	27 .479	1995	27 .594	1999	39 .572
1992	43*.529	1996	47 .643		*led league

Also: Has the five highest single-season home run totals, and three of the top single-season RBI totals, in Rangers history; was the fifth fastest to reach 300 career homers. Has the second-highest RBI total at the All-Star break, 101 in 1998, and his 157 that season is the 11th-highest in history.

"He's easy to pitch to. But so was Babe Ruth."

— Scout Hugh Alexander

Home Runs/Slugging%			
1985	4 .527	1993	30 .464
1986	4 .325	1994	28 .504
1987	14 .560	1995	31 .472
1988	9 .431	1996	39 .484
1990	51* .592*	1997	13 .410
1991	44* .513	1998	17 .401
1992	35 .458	*led league	

Also: Won back-to-back home run titles and three consecutive RBI titles 1990-92.

Momentous clouts

He became the third righthanded hitter to clear the left-field roof at Tiger Stadium on August 25, 1990, off Oakland's Dave Stewart. On October 3, 1990, he smashed home runs Nos. 50 and 51 in a 10-3 victory over the Yankees, making him the first player in 13 seasons to break the 50-home run barrier.

Big Daddy

31
CECIL
FIELDER

6-3, 240 Career HRs: 319 Career slugging percentage: .482 HR-to-hit ratio: 1 to

"I've seen him hit a home run off his front foot. I've seen him hit a line drive over the center field fence, 440 feet."

—Mickey Tettleton

Kong

You

Momentous clouts

He hit three tape-measure homers out of
Wrigley Field in the memorable 11-homer,
23-22 Phillies-Cubs game on May 17th,
1979. Hit five homers in a two-game span
to tie a major-league record in 1979, and
twice hit three homers in a game in 1979.

32 DAVE KINGM

6-6, 220 Career HRs: 442 Career slugging percentage: .478 HR-to-hit ratio: 1 to

Home Runs/Slugging% *led league

75	36 .494	1977	20 .444	1979	48*.613*	1981	22 .456	1983	13 .383	1985	30 .417
76	37 .506	1978	28 .542	1980	18 .522	1982	37*.432	1984	35 .505	1986	35 .431

Also: Won home run and slugging percentage titles in 1979.

"I'd rather hit home runs.
don't have to run as hard."

—*Dave Kingman*

3.56 HR-to-AB ratio: 1 every 15.1 at-bats   **TSNdex power ranking: 171.3**

Also: Won four home-run titles, two RBI titles and one slugging percentage title in a five-year period from 1926-30. Had a major-league record 190 RBIs in 1930, a record that stands to this day.

Momentous clouts

On September 27, 1930, Wilson hits home runs No. 55 and 56 against the Cincinnati Reds, establishing a National League record that would stand for 68 years.

33 LEWIS HACK WILSON

5-6, 195 Career HRs: 244 Career slugging percentage: .545 HR-to-hit ratio: 1 to

"Hack hit one in Cincinnati one day, hit it so hard that it hit the screen and bounced back on the field. The umpire thought it hit the fence below the screen and ruled it a double. I was sitting in the Cincinnati bullpen, and of course we weren't going to say anything."

—*Reds pitcher Clyde Sukeforth on what should have been Wilson's 57th homer in 1930*

Hack Wilson

"From the elbows down, he's got the muscle of a 230-pounder."

—Pitcher Robin Roberts

34

Mr. Cub

ERNIE
BANKS

6-1, 186 Career HRs: 512 Career slugging percentage: .500 HR-to-hit ratio: 1 to

Year	HR	Slugging%
1953	2	.571
1954	19	.427
1955	44	.596
1956	28	.530
1957	43	.579
1958	47*	.614*
1959	45	.596
1960	41*	.554
1961	29	.507
1962	37	.503
1963	18	.403
1964	23	.450
1965	28	.453
1966	15	.432
1967	23	.455
1968	32	.469
1969	23	.416
1970	12	.459
1971	3	.325

led league

Also: Hit 40-plus homers five times in six-year span 1955-60, and led the majors in homers over that period.

Momentous clouts

On his way to a then-record 44 homers by a shortstop in 1955, he hit three in one game at Wrigley Field against Pittsburgh. A blast on May 12, 1970, not only was his 500th career homer, but his 1,600th RBI as well. He would hit only 12 more homers and drive in 36 more runs over the next one-plus seasons.

5.04 HR-to-AB ratio: 1 every 18.4 at-bats   TSNdex power ranking: 179.1   79

Home Runs/ Slugging%		
1957	14	.405
1958	28	.431
1959	16	.464
1960	39	.581*
1961	61*	.620
1962	33	.485
1963	23	.542
1964	26	.464
1965	8	.439
1966	13	.382
1967	9	.405
1968	5	.374

* led league

"Why shouldn't he break Ruth's record?

He's got more power than Stalin."

—*Manager Casey Stengel during the 1961 season*

Also: Won the MVP award, RBI title and slugging percentage title in season before he broke Ruth's home run record. Led the league in runs scored in 61-homer season.

35 ROGER

6-0, 205 Career HRs: 275 Career slugging percentage: .476 HR-to-hit ratio: 1 to

Until Mark McGwire, arguably the most memorable home run in history came on October 1, 1961, the final day of the season in Yankee Stadium. Numbers 37, 38, 39 and 40 in his historic season all came on the same day, July 25, 1961, in a doubleheader against Chicago.

Momentous clouts

MARIS

4.81 HR-to-AB ratio: 1 every 18.5 at-bats   TSNdex power ranking: 167.1

36
DICK ALLEN

"As for the best player I ever played with at the peak of his talent, Richie
year. I won 21 games that year, and Richie won at least 10 of them for me

Home Runs/Slugging%
* led league

1963	0	.458	1968	33	.520	1973	16	.612
1964	29	.557	1969	32	.573	1974	32*	.563*
1965	20	.494	1970	34	.560	1975	12	.385
1966	40	.632*	1971	23	.468	1976	15	.480
1967	23	.566	1972	37*	.603*	1977	5	.351

Also: Won home run, RBI and slugging percentage titles in 1972, one other home run title and two slugging percentage titles.

Allen in 1972, when he was the MVP, was the best. He had an incredible with his bat. He was the most feared hitter in the league." —*pitcher Stan Bahnsen*

Momentous clouts

He is one of only four players to hit the center-field bleachers in the old Comiskey Park.

5.3 HR-to-AB ratio: 1 every 18.0 at-bats

TSNdex power ranking: 197.8

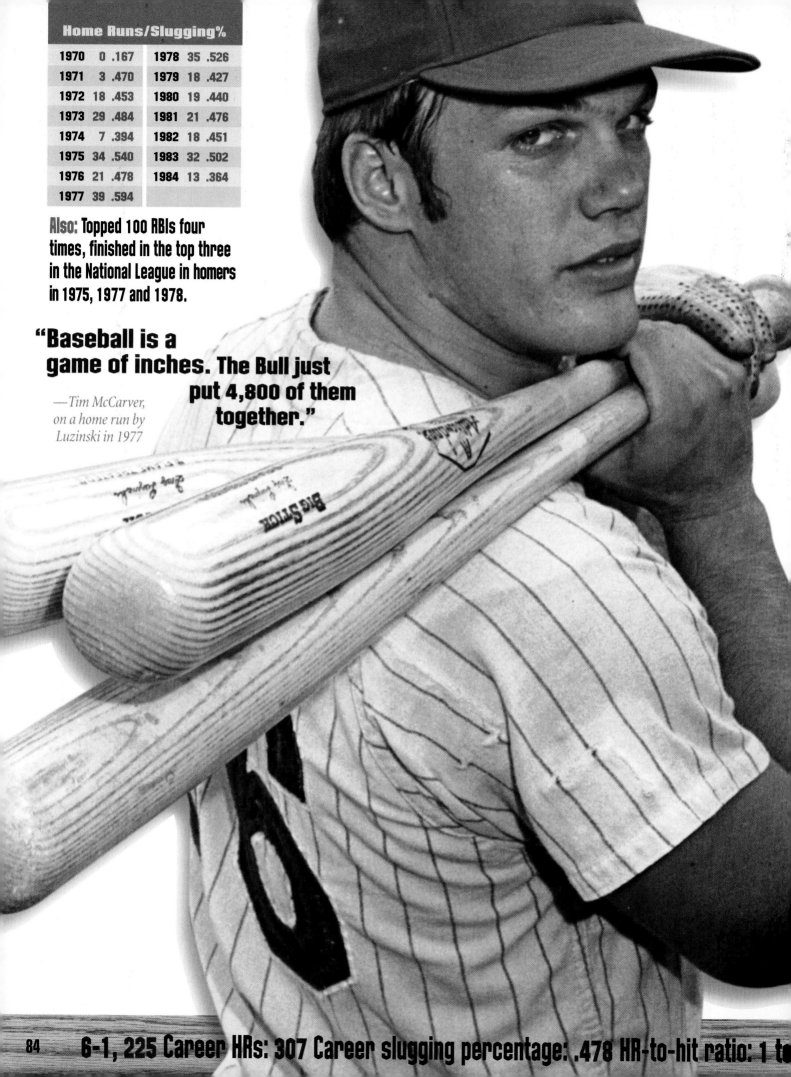

Home Runs/Slugging%

Year	HR	SLG	Year	HR	SLG
1970	0	.167	1978	35	.526
1971	3	.470	1979	18	.427
1972	18	.453	1980	19	.440
1973	29	.484	1981	21	.476
1974	7	.394	1982	18	.451
1975	34	.540	1983	32	.502
1976	21	.478	1984	13	.364
1977	39	.594			

Also: Topped 100 RBIs four times, finished in the top three in the National League in homers in 1975, 1977 and 1978.

"Baseball is a game of inches. The Bull just put 4,800 of them together."

—Tim McCarver, on a home run by Luzinski in 1977

6-1, 225 Career HRs: 307 Career slugging percentage: .478 HR-to-hit ratio: 1 t

Momentous clouts

His first major-league homer, off Reggie Cleveland on September 7, 1971, landed in the upper deck at Philadelphia's Veterans Stadium. He would hit nine more up there in his career, most in stadium history. He also hit four home runs in three NLCS series from 1976-78.

GREG
LUZINSKI

37

"The first man in the history of the game to be killed by a batted ball will be an innocent stranger. He will be walking down the street in back of Crosley Field, and he will be hit on the head by a ball driven out of the park by Ted Kluszewski."

—*Umpire Larry Goetz*

38 TEDKLU

6-2, 240 Career HRs: 279 Career slugging percentage: .498 HR-to-hit ratio: 1 to

Home Runs/Slugging%

| 1947 | 0 | .100 | 1949 | 8 | .411 | 1951 | 13 | .387 | 1953 | 40 | .570 | 1955 | 47 | .585 | 1957 | 6 | .465 | 1959 | 2 | .410 | 1961 | 15 | .460 |
| 1948 | 12 | .451 | 1950 | 25 | .515 | 1952 | 16 | .509 | 1954 | 49* | .642 | 1956 | 35 | .536 | 1958 | 4 | .402 | 1960 | 5 | .425 | *led league | | |

Momentous clouts

In Game 1 of the 1959 World Series, Kluszewski drove in five runs with a pair of two-run homers and a run-scoring single for the "Go-Go" White Sox, who would go on to lose the first Series played on the West Coast to the Los Angeles Dodgers. Klu finished his one and only World Series appearance with three homers and 10 RBIs.

"Kluszewski? Hell, I thought we were talking about human beings."

—Manager Leo Durocher, when asked why he omitted Kluszewski in his answer to the question of who was the strongest man in the National League

Kluszewski's biceps were a source of power and amusement for the White Sox and teammates Luis Aparicio and Nellie Fox.

SZEWSKI

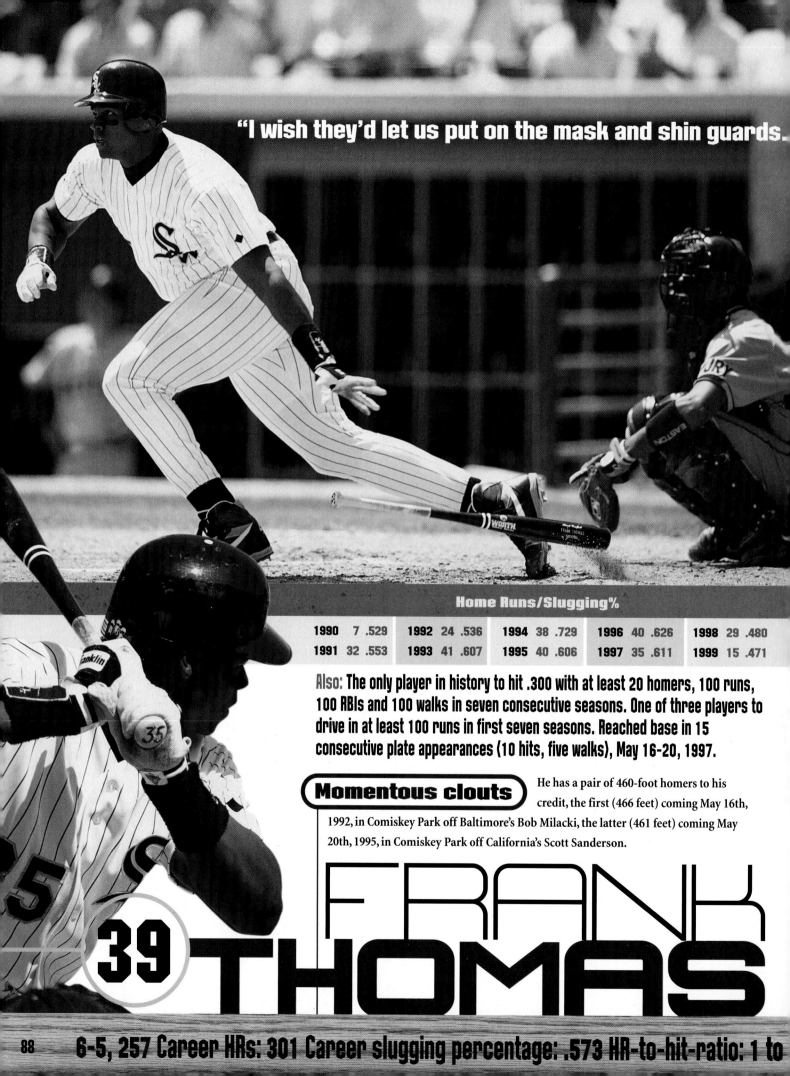

"I wish they'd let us put on the mask and shin guards.

Home Runs/Slugging%

| 1990 | 7 | .529 | 1992 | 24 | .536 | 1994 | 38 | .729 | 1996 | 40 | .626 | 1998 | 29 | .480 |
| 1991 | 32 | .553 | 1993 | 41 | .607 | 1995 | 40 | .606 | 1997 | 35 | .611 | 1999 | 15 | .471 |

Also: The only player in history to hit .300 with at least 20 homers, 100 runs, 100 RBIs and 100 walks in seven consecutive seasons. One of three players to drive in at least 100 runs in first seven seasons. Reached base in 15 consecutive plate appearances (10 hits, five walks), May 16-20, 1997.

Momentous clouts He has a pair of 460-foot homers to his credit, the first (466 feet) coming May 16th, 1992, in Comiskey Park off Baltimore's Bob Milacki, the latter (461 feet) coming May 20th, 1995, in Comiskey Park off California's Scott Sanderson.

FRANK THOMAS
39

6-5, 257 Career HRs: 301 Career slugging percentage: .573 HR-to-hit-ratio: 1 to

Pitchers shouldn't be left out there alone with him."
—Pitcher Dennis Martinez

The Big Hurt

40

Home Runs/ Slugging%		
1967	1	.256
1968	15	.433
1969	26	.487
1970	45*	.587
1971	27	.423
1972	40*	.541
1973	25	.429
1974	33	.507
1975	28	.519
1976	16	.394
1977	31	.540
1978	23	.483
1979	22	.459
1980	24	.483
1981	8	.489
1982	13	.396

led league

Also: Won two home run titles and three RBI titles 1970-74. All-time leader in home runs by a catcher.

Hands

6-1, 208 Career HRs: 389 Career slugging percentage: .476 HR-to-hit ratio: 1 to

"Don't embarrass nobody by comparing him to Johnny Bench. I don't believe to this day that you can compare anybody to Johnny Bench."

— *Sparky Anderson*

JOHNNY BENCH

Momentous clouts

He hit three homers on July 26, 1970, en route to setting a then-record of 36 by July 31. Had two other three-homer games, May 9, 1973, and May 29, 1980. He hit seven homers in five games from May 30 to June 3, 1972. Belted home runs in the 1969, 1971 and 1973 All-Star games.

5.3 HR-to-AB ratio: 1 every 19.7 at-bats

TSNdex power ranking: 161.7

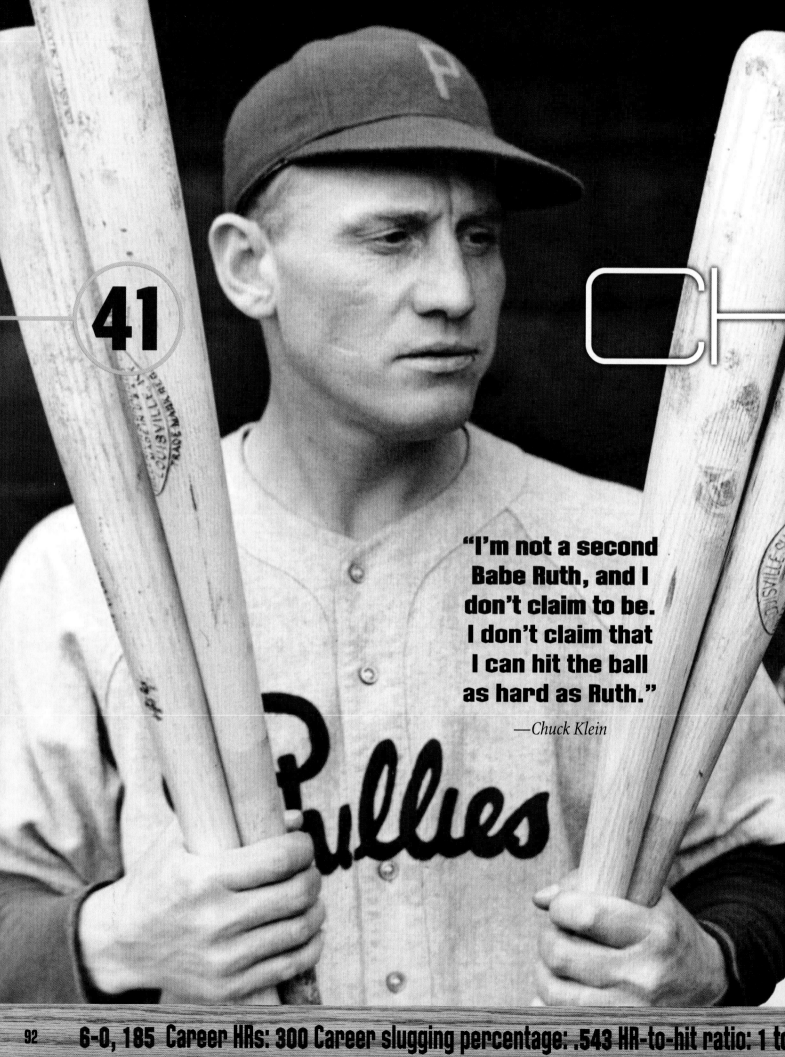

CH

"I'm not a second Babe Ruth, and I don't claim to be. I don't claim that I can hit the ball as hard as Ruth."

—*Chuck Klein*

6-0, 185 Career HRs: 300 Career slugging percentage: .543 HR-to-hit ratio: 1 to

1928	11	.577	1931	31*	.584*	1934	20	.510	1937	15	.495	1940	7	.333	1943	0	.100
1929	43*	.657	1932	38*	.646*	1935	21	.488	1938	8	.356	1941	1	.164	1944	0	.143
1930	40	.687	1933	28*	.602*	1936	25	.512	1939	12	.486	1942	0	.071	*led league		

Also: Won the N.L. Triple Crown in 1933; won the N.L. home run and slugging percentage titles from 1931-33; had 200 or more hits in five consecutive seasons 1929-33; and led the league in total bases from 1930-33.

Momentous clouts

On July 10, 1936, he hit four homers in a 10-inning game.

He hit six homers in a four-game stretch in 1929.

CHUCK KLEIN

HALL OF FAME: 1980

> "Every time he swings,
> **I cringe.**
> Every time he fouls one off,
> **I shudder.**"
>
> —*Birdie Tebbetts*

JOHN
BOOG
POWELL

Momentous clouts

Hit three homers in a game three times:
August 10, 1963, June 27, 1964 and August
15, 1966. Hit two home runs in the 1970
World Series, and two homers in the
second game of the 1971 American League
Championship Series.

6-4, 240 Career HRs: 339 Career slugging percentage: .462 HR-to-hit ratio: 1 to

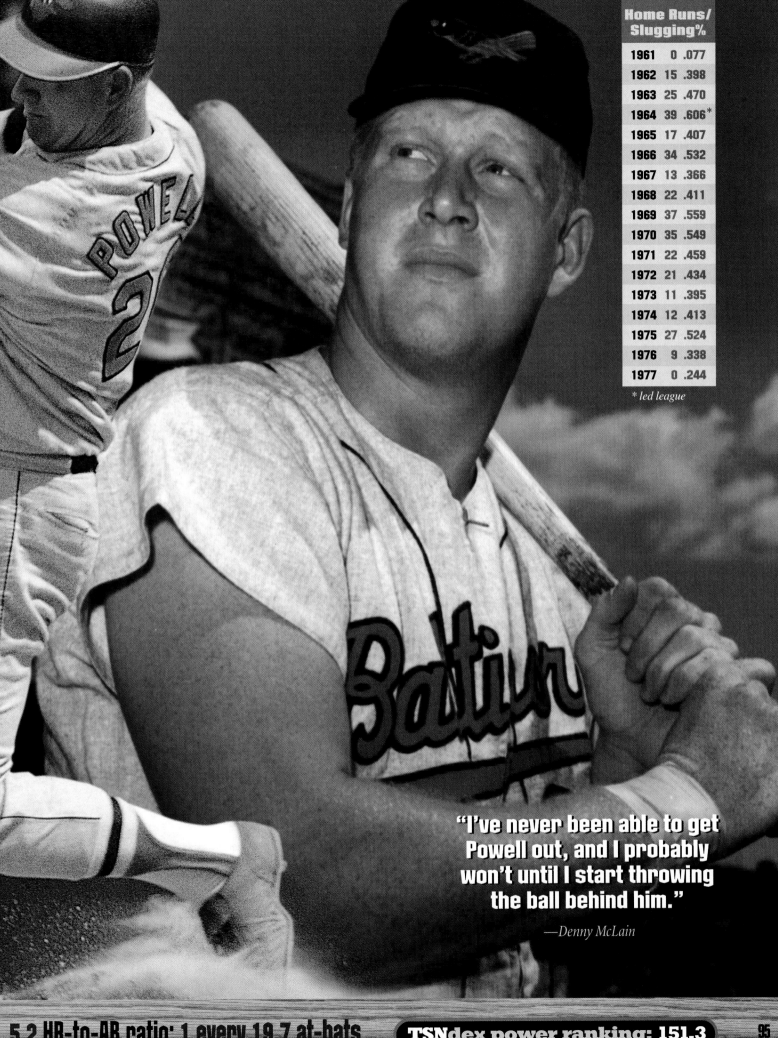

Home Runs/ Slugging%		
1961	0	.077
1962	15	.398
1963	25	.470
1964	39	.606*
1965	17	.407
1966	34	.532
1967	13	.366
1968	22	.411
1969	37	.559
1970	35	.549
1971	22	.459
1972	21	.434
1973	11	.395
1974	12	.413
1975	27	.524
1976	9	.338
1977	0	.244

* led league

"I've never been able to get Powell out, and I probably won't until I start throwing the ball behind him."

—Denny McLain

5.2 HR-to-AB ratio: 1 every 19.7 at-bats

TSNdex power ranking: 151.3

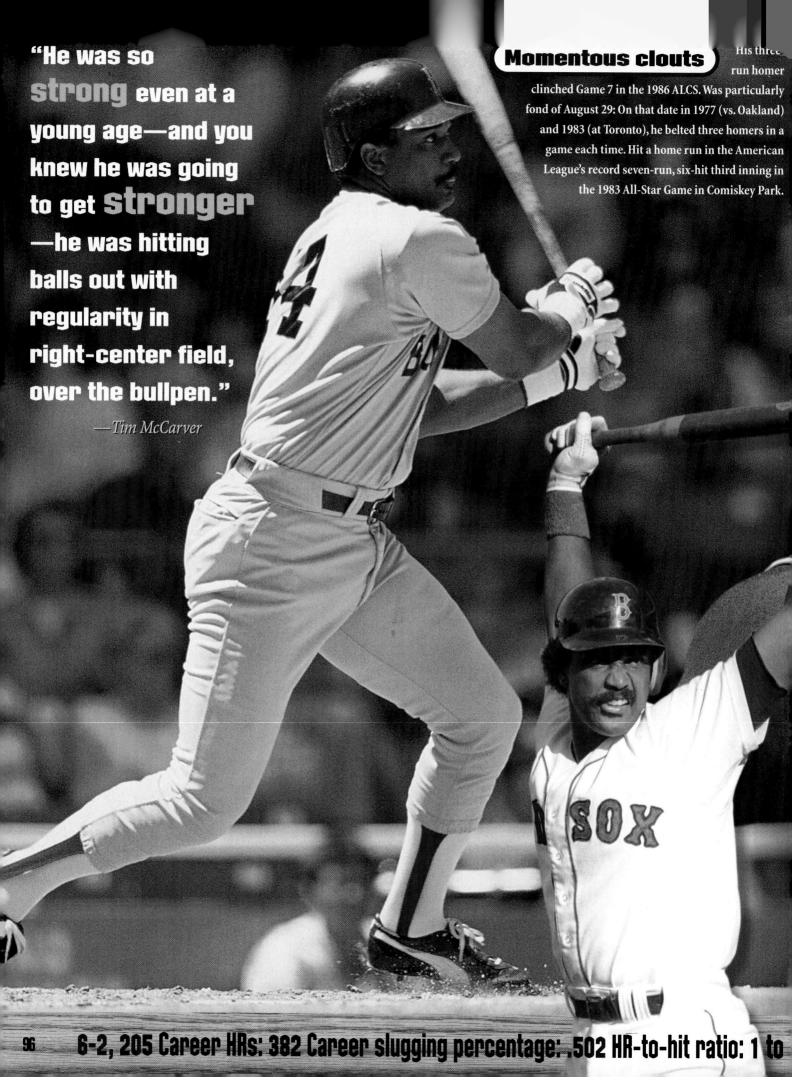

"He was so **strong** even at a young age—and you knew he was going to get **stronger** —he was hitting balls out with regularity in right-center field, over the bullpen."

—*Tim McCarver*

His three run homer clinched Game 7 in the 1986 ALCS. Was particularly fond of August 29: On that date in 1977 (vs. Oakland) and 1983 (at Toronto), he belted three homers in a game each time. Hit a home run in the American League's record seven-run, six-hit third inning in the 1983 All-Star Game in Comiskey Park.

6-2, 205 Career HRs: 382 Career slugging percentage: .502 HR-to-hit ratio: 1 to

Also: Won three home run titles, two RBI titles and two slugging percentage titles, hit 39 or more homers four times 1977-83. His 406 total bases in 1978 were the most in the A.L. since Joe DiMaggio's 418 in 1937. Was the first player with three consecutive 35-homer/200-hit seasons, 1977-79.

	Home Runs/ Slugging%	
1974	1	.373
1975	22	.491
1976	25	.482
1977	39*	.593*
1978	46*	.600*
1979	39	.596
1980	24	.504
1981	17	.441
1982	24	.494
1983	39*	.550
1984	28	.467
1985	27	.487
1986	20	.490
1987	13	.408
1988	15	.406
1989	3	.344

led league

43 JIM RICE

6.4 HR-to-AB ratio: 1 every 21.5 at-bats

TSNdex power ranking: 174.3

Hit three homers on July 14, 1977, and a then-National League record 31 on the road that season. Belted six of the first 13 homers that reached the upper level of Riverfront Stadium/Cynergy Field.

Momentous clouts

"You can turn your back and still know when Foster is hitting in batting practice. There is a different ring when he hits a ball."

—*Reds manager Sparky Anderson in 1976*

FO

6-1, 185 Career HRs: 348 Career slugging percentage: .480 HR-to-hit ratio: 1 to

1969	0	.400	1978	40*	.546
1970	1	.632	1979	30	.561
1971	13	.389	1980	25	.473
1972	2	.283	1981	22	.519
1973	4	.667	1982	13	.367
1974	7	.406	1983	28	.419
1975	23	.518	1984	24	.443
1976	29	.530	1985	21	.460
1977	52*	.631*	1986	14	.415

Also: Won three consecutive RBI titles from 1976-78, home run titles in 1977-78 and a slugging title in 1977 when he was the first National Leaguer in 12 years and only the seventh all-time to hit 50 homers. Averaged 32 homers and 107 RBIs from 1975-81. In 1977, fell just one RBI and three hits shy of becoming only the fourth player to hit .300 with 200 hits, 50 homers and 150 RBIs in a season

44 GEORGE

.53 HR-to-AB ratio: 1 every 20.2 at-bats

Winny

Momentous clouts

His two-run double in the 11th inning of Game 6 of the World Series gave the Toronto Blue Jays a 4-3 Series-clinching win. He hit three homers in a game April 13, 1991.

45

6-6, 220 Career HRs: 465 Career slugging percentage: .475 HR-to-hit ratio: 1 to

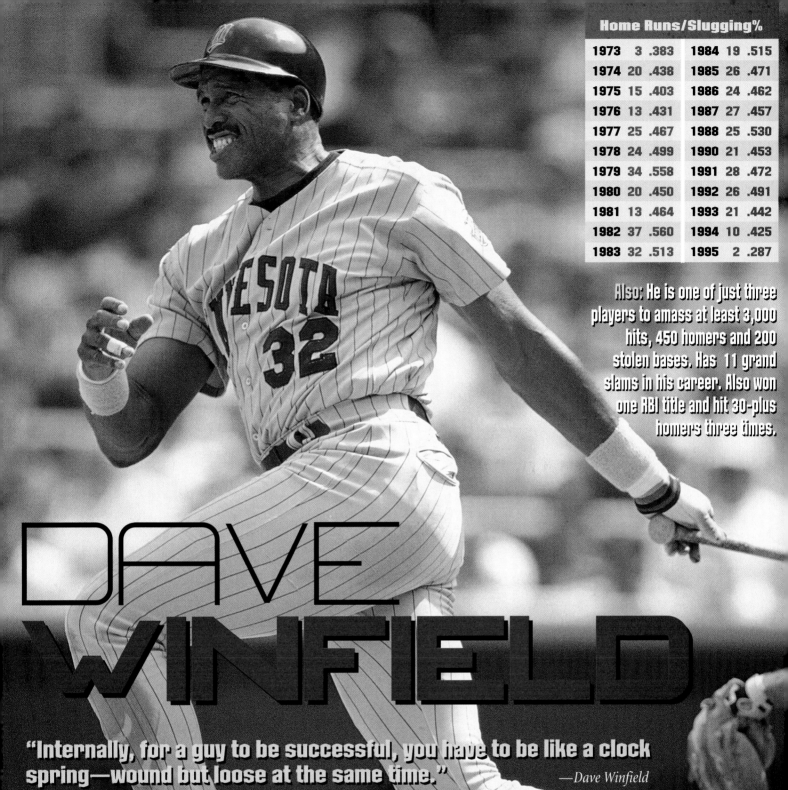

Home Runs/Slugging%			
1973	3 .383	1984	19 .515
1974	20 .438	1985	26 .471
1975	15 .403	1986	24 .462
1976	13 .431	1987	27 .457
1977	25 .467	1988	25 .530
1978	24 .499	1990	21 .453
1979	34 .558	1991	28 .472
1980	20 .450	1992	26 .491
1981	13 .464	1993	21 .442
1982	37 .560	1994	10 .425
1983	32 .513	1995	2 .287

Also: He is one of just three players to amass at least 3,000 hits, 450 homers and 200 stolen bases. Has 11 grand slams in his career. Also won one RBI title and hit 30-plus homers three times.

DAVE WINFIELD

"Internally, for a guy to be successful, you have to be like a clock spring—wound but loose at the same time."
—Dave Winfield

6.7 HR-to-AB ratio: 1 every 23.7 at-bats

TSNdex power ranking: 160.4

101

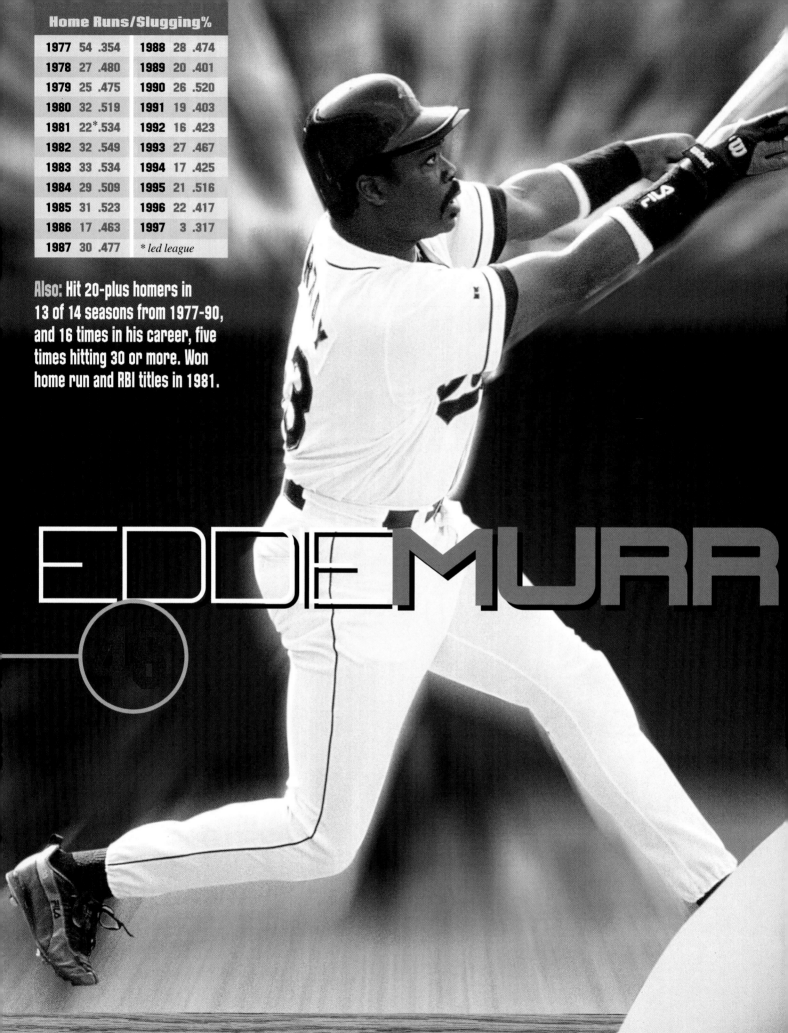

Home Runs/Slugging%

1977	54	.354	**1988**	28	.474
1978	27	.480	**1989**	20	.401
1979	25	.475	**1990**	26	.520
1980	32	.519	**1991**	19	.403
1981	22*	.534	**1992**	16	.423
1982	32	.549	**1993**	27	.467
1983	33	.534	**1994**	17	.425
1984	29	.509	**1995**	21	.516
1985	31	.523	**1996**	22	.417
1986	17	.463	**1997**	3	.317
1987	30	.477	*led league		

Also: Hit 20-plus homers in 13 of 14 seasons from 1977-90, and 16 times in his career, five times hitting 30 or more. Won home run and RBI titles in 1981.

EDDIE MURR

6-2, 204 Career HRs: 504 Career slugging percentage: .476 HR-to-hit ratio: 1 to

"Other people may disagree, but if you're asking me what player I'd want up there to win a game for me, it's Eddie Murray."

—*Sparky Anderson*

Momentous clouts

No switch-hitter has had more games with homers from both sides of the plate (11), including two in three different seasons. He hit 19 career grand slams, and three homers in a game three times.

ANDRE DAWSON

"He came up in situations and took over. If he needed a home run, he got a home run. If he needed a hit, he got a hit." — *Manager Jim Frey*

Also: Hit .300 or better five times, drove in 100 or more runs four times, won N.L home run and RBI titles and the Most Valuable Player award in 1987, led the N.L. in total bases in 1983 and 1987.

Home Runs/Slugging%

Year	HR	Slug%	Year	HR	Slug%	Year	HR	Slug%	Year	HR	Slug%
1976	0	.306	1982	23	.498	1988	24	.504	1994	16	.466
1977	19	.474	1983	32	.539	1989	21	.476	1995	8	.434
1978	25	.442	1984	17	.409	1990	27	.535	1996	2	.414
1979	25	.468	1985	23	.444	1991	31	.488	*led league		
1980	17	.492	1986	20	.478	1992	22	.456			
1981	24	.553	1987	49*	.568	1993	13	.425			

6-3, 195 Career HRs: 438 Career slugging percentage: .482 HR-to-hit ratio: 1 to

47

Hit three homers, drove in eight runs, and tied major-league records with two homers and six RBIs in one inning on September 24, 1985. Hit home runs in three consecutive at-bats, August 1, 1987. Reached the upper deck in the Astrodome on April 16, 1983. Hit five homers in a three-game span twice in 1987.

Momentous clouts

6.33 HR-to-AB ratio: 1 every 22.7 at-bats

TSNdex power ranking: 167.2

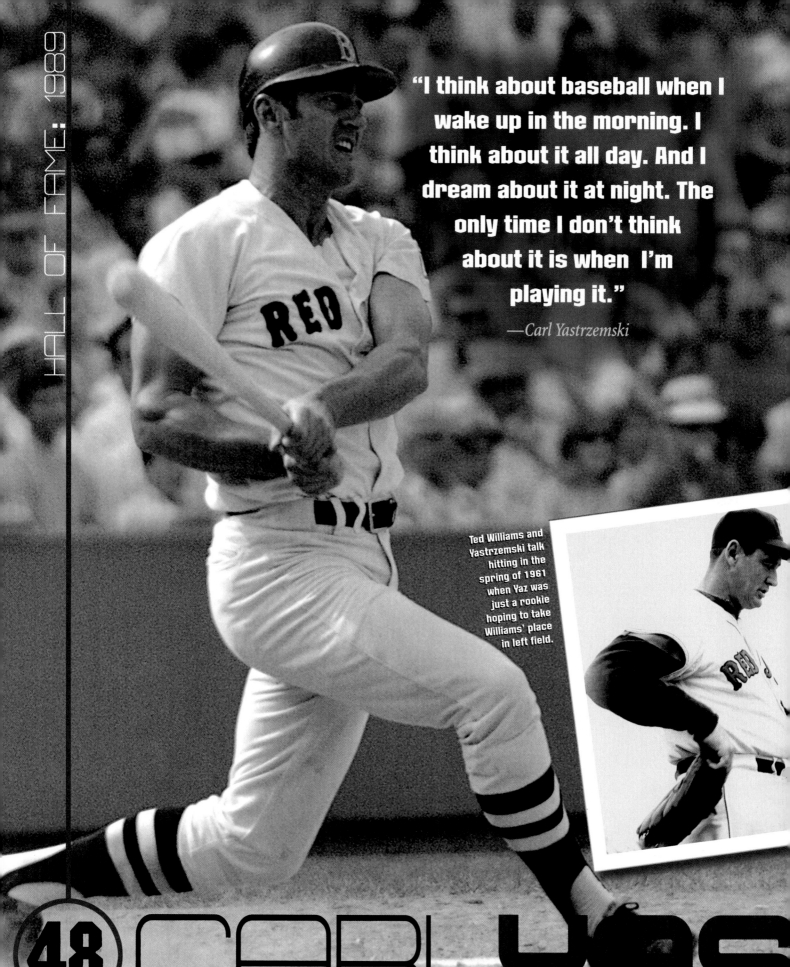

"I think about baseball when I wake up in the morning. I think about it all day. And I dream about it at night. The only time I don't think about it is when I'm playing it."

—*Carl Yastrzemski*

Ted Williams and Yastrzemski talk hitting in the spring of 1961 when Yaz was just a rookie hoping to take Williams' place in left field.

(48) CARL YAS

5-11, 182 Career HRs: 452 Career slugging percentage: .462 HR-to-hit ratio: 1 to

1961	11	.396	1964	15	.451	1967	44*	.622*	1970	40	.592*	1973	19	.463	1976	21	.432	1979	21	.450	1982	16	.431
1962	19	.469	1965	20	.536*	1968	23	.495	1971	15	.392	1974	15	.445	1977	28	.505	1980	15	.462	1983	10	.408
1963	14	.475	1966	16	.431	1969	40	.507	1972	12	.391	1975	14	.405	1978	17	.423	1981	7	.355			*led league

Also: The majors' last Triple Crown winner. Hit 40 or more homers three times from 1967-70, with two slugging percentage titles and one RBI title.

Momentous clouts

His 44th and final home run in 1967 tied him with Harmon Killebrew and gave him the Triple Crown. He hit three homers in the 1967 World Series, and a home run off Ron Guidry in the Yankees-Red Sox 1978 playoff game.

TRZEMSKI

.6 HR-to-AB ratio: 1 every 26.5 at-bats

TSNdex power ranking: 148.1

DALE MU

Momentous clouts

Tied a major-league record with two home runs and drove in six runs in the sixth inning on July 27, 1989. Hit three home runs on May 18, 1979, at San Francisco. Homered in the 1984 All-Star Game.

6-5, 215 Career HRs: 398 Career slugging percentage: .469 HR-to-hit ratio: 1 t

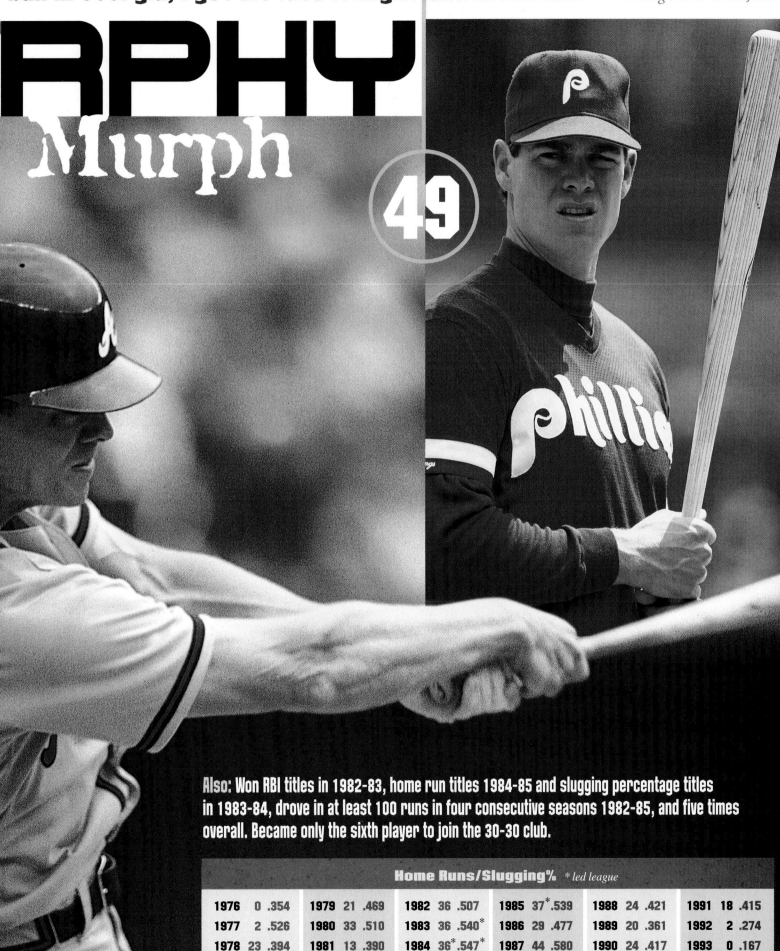

RPHY
Murph

49

Also: Won RBI titles in 1982-83, home run titles 1984-85 and slugging percentage titles in 1983-84, drove in at least 100 runs in four consecutive seasons 1982-85, and five times overall. Became only the sixth player to join the 30-30 club.

Home Runs/Slugging% *led league*

1976	0 .354	1979	21 .469	1982	36 .507	1985	37* .539	1988	24 .421	1991	18 .415
1977	2 .526	1980	33 .510	1983	36 .540*	1986	29 .477	1989	20 .361	1992	2 .274
1978	23 .394	1981	13 .390	1984	36* .547*	1987	44 .580	1990	24 .417	1993	0 .167

5.3 HR-to-AB ratio: 1 every 20 at-bats

TSNdex power ranking: 157.3

"You know that highlight reel that shows the grabs his head with his hands in amazement?

Momentous clouts

Is one of only 19 players to hit grand slams in consecutive games (August 13-14, 1991). Hit two home runs in both the 1995 and 1996 World Series. His dramatic two-run, ninth-inning homer off Lee Smith tied the 1994 All-Star Game and won him the Most Valuable Player Award for the game.

Crime Dog

50 FRE

6-3, 215 Career HRs: 390 Career slugging percentage: .517 HR-to-hit ratio: 1 to

Willie Mays catch and then switches to the fan, who Fred McGriff does that to you when he hits a home run."

—*Toronto teammate Lloyd Moseby in 1989*

"When he comes up, we hold our breath."

—*Rangers manager Bobby Valentine in 1989*

Also: Is one of only nine players to hit 30 or more homers in seven consecutive seasons (1988-94), and the only one to do it while changing leagues. The other eight are in the Hall of Fame. Hit 20 or more in 11 consecutive seasons, 1987-97. First player in the modern era to lead both leagues in homers.

Home Runs/Slugging%			
1986	0 .200	1993	37 .549
1987	20 .505	1994	34 .623
1988	34 .552	1995	27 .489
1989	36* .525	1996	28 .494
1990	35 .530	1997	22 .441
1991	31 .494	1998	19 443
1992	35* .556	1999	32 .552

* led league

McGRIFF

4.99 HR-to-AB ratio: 1 every 17.4 at-bats   **TSNdex power ranking: 179.3**

Jake Beckley

TRIPL

THREAT

So you think there is too much offense in Major League Baseball at the dawn of the new millennium? That's open to debate, but what's going on in the game today really is nothing more than a repeat of history. The last time a new century dawned, the story was similar.

The 1890s marked a time in the game's unsettled infancy when the established National League held off challenges from far-flung organizations such as the American Association, the Union Association and the Players League. No fewer than 26 cities had a "major-league" designation at one point or another—although the 1899 Cleveland Spiders pushed that envelope by finishing 20-134, 84 games behind the Brooklyn Superbas.

Between the white lines, the action was equally chaotic— racked by gambling and cheating, and clearly dominated by hitting. Pitchers threw submarine style from flat ground to a 12-inch-wide square home plate, and hitters simply teed off, aided by the advantage of not having foul balls count as strikes and fielders wearing inadequate gloves.

Unlike the 1990s, there weren't many home runs. More often than not, games were played in stadiums with wooden grandstands and outfield walls that were nothing more than where the line of spectators began. The triple—not the home run—was the power number of importance, and the 1894 Baltimore Orioles hit 150 of them in a 129-game season.

It's also no coincidence that of the top 20 all-time triples leaders, three played their entire careers before 1900, eight more played before the

The 1890s was a time when Wee Willie Keeler, all 5-4 and 140 pounds of him, was 'keeping his eyes clear and hittin' 'em where they ain't.'

turn of the century, and seven more began their careers within the first 15 years of the 1900s. The names Jake Beckley, Roger Connor, Fred Clarke, Dan Brouthers and Joe Kelley may be unfamiliar to all but the most ardent fans and historians of the game, but their names have stood in the record book among the top 10 in three-baggers for a century.

Back then, the defense against the longball simply was to play deep, which led to hits falling in everywhere and runs in bushels—Coors Field-like averages of 13.1 per game in 1893, 14.7 per game in 1894 and 13.2 per game in 1895. John McGraw, long before he began a legendary managing career, led the league in runs scored in 1898 and 1899 with 143 and 140, and stolen base king "Slidin' Billy" Hamilton did so four times with totals of 141 (1891), 152 (1897), 166 (1895) and an amazing 192 in 1894.

This was a time when "Wee Willie" Keeler, all 5-4 and 140 pounds of him, was keeping his eyes clear and hittin' 'em where they ain't. He had 200 or more hits in eight consecutive years 1894-1901, and never played in more than 141 games in a season. He never batted below .362 in that stretch, and won a batting title in 1897 with a .424 average, and another in 1898 at .385.

A .400 batting average wasn't a sacred milestone, but merely a target for the elite hitters of the day. It was reached 11 times from 1894 through 1901, including by no fewer than five players in 1894, led by Boston's Hugh Duffy at .440. Cleveland's Jesse Burkett hit .400 in back-to-back seasons in 1895 and 1896. But each time, he found himself in a battle for the batting title,

Long before he became a legendary manager, John McGraw (above in his playing days and below as a manager) led the league in runs scored in 1898 and 1899 for Baltimore.

edging Philadelphia's Ed Delahanty and then Baltimore's Hughie Jennings. Teams hit .300 with regularity, the National League average was .309 in 1894.

No pre-1900 season was more offensive than 1894. The Phillies batted .349 as a team, six points higher than Baltimore. Eight of the National League's 12 teams hit better than .300. Boston slugged 103 homers, the only team in the decade to reach 100. Boston's Bobby Lowe became the first major-league player to hit four homers in a game that season. To go with his .440 average, Triple Crown winner Duffy belted 51 doubles, 16 triples and 18 homers, and drove in 145 runs—all in 125 games and 539 at-bats. Six teams hit 100 or more triples. The league ERA that season was 5.32, only two teams were below 5.00, and it would have been worse if not for New York's Amos Rusie, the game's first fireballer.

In 1894, Rusie, "The Hoosier Thunderbolt" was 36-13 with a 2.78 ERA, almost 2½ runs below the league average. He won 246 games in a 10-year span, completed 392-of-427 starts, and averaged 416 innings and a 3.07 ERA. But for all that success, Rusie averaged only 4.6 strikeouts per nine innings due to the era's emphasis on contact hitting.

Along with the ultra-high averages of the

TRIPLE THREAT

Cap Anson (above) was a mainstay with a bat in Chicago in the late 19th century, while Boston's Bobby Lowe (left) became the first major-leaguer to hit four homers in a game. He did that in consecutive at-bats vs. Cincinnati in 1894.

decade came liberal use of the running game. Beginning in 1894. Hamilton had single-season stolen-base totals of 98, 97, 83, 66 and 54 and finished in the league's top three each of those seasons. McGraw and his Orioles teammates ran up astronomical league-leading stolen-base totals of 441 in 1896, 401 in 1897 and 364 in 1899. Many years later, near the end of McGraw's brilliant run as a manager, he lamented a passing of that style of play: "... the thrill of seeing men shoot down the base paths, one after another, until they had stolen their way to a win. That was baseball—the kind of baseball I learned to love ... "

Home runs? With thick-handled bats that weighed up to three pounds, hitters valued placement, not power. The perennial league

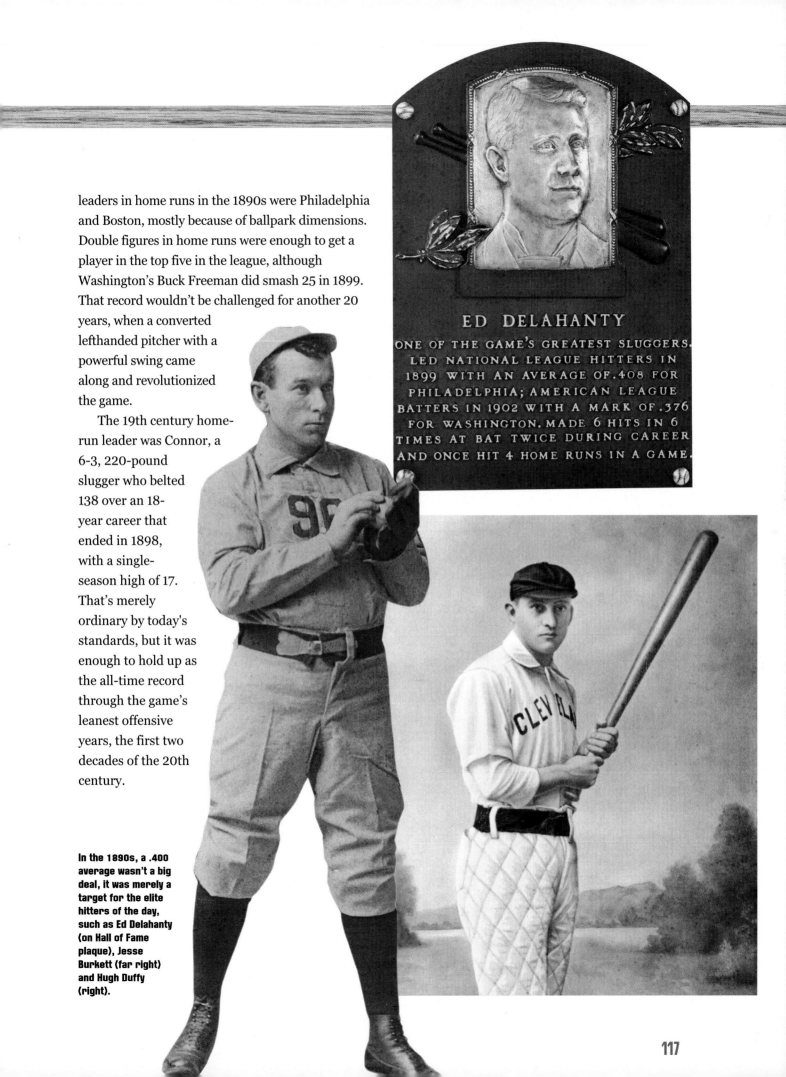

leaders in home runs in the 1890s were Philadelphia and Boston, mostly because of ballpark dimensions. Double figures in home runs were enough to get a player in the top five in the league, although Washington's Buck Freeman did smash 25 in 1899. That record wouldn't be challenged for another 20 years, when a converted lefthanded pitcher with a powerful swing came along and revolutionized the game.

The 19th century home-run leader was Connor, a 6-3, 220-pound slugger who belted 138 over an 18-year career that ended in 1898, with a single-season high of 17. That's merely ordinary by today's standards, but it was enough to hold up as the all-time record through the game's leanest offensive years, the first two decades of the 20th century.

In the 1890s, a .400 average wasn't a big deal, it was merely a target for the elite hitters of the day, such as Ed Delahanty (on Hall of Fame plaque), Jesse Burkett (far right) and Hugh Duffy (right).

ED DELAHANTY

ONE OF THE GAME'S GREATEST SLUGGERS. LED NATIONAL LEAGUE HITTERS IN 1899 WITH AN AVERAGE OF .408 FOR PHILADELPHIA; AMERICAN LEAGUE BATTERS IN 1902 WITH A MARK OF .376 FOR WASHINGTON. MADE 6 HITS IN 6 TIMES AT BAT TWICE DURING CAREER AND ONCE HIT 4 HOME RUNS IN A GAME.

Ty Cobb,
Detroit Tigers

THE DEAD

His nickname was 'Home Run', but Frank Baker hit only 96 in his career. The moniker came from two big homers he hit in the 1911 World Series, which followed a season in which he led the American League with 11 homers.

It seems logical

now that foul balls be counted as strikes up to strike two. But the hitters of the early 1900s complained loudly when the rule was put into effect. And with that simple but momentous change, the game began to change.

The National League made the switch in 1901, the newly established American League followed in 1903, both hoping to speed up games. Coupled with other happenings of the era—mushy baseballs that were used for most of a game, pitchers throwing overhand and from a raised mound, and the use of spitballs and other substances— the combination silenced offenses more effectively than Sandy Koufax on a good day.

American League scoring dropped from 5,407 runs in 1902 to 4,543 in 1903, or 16 percent. The league ERA fell from 3.57 to 2.96. In a two-year span, National League run

Detroit's Sam Crawford was the prototypical Deadball Era slugger— more prolific at doubles and triples than homers.

production dropped from 10.4 runs per game in 1900 to 8.0 in 1902, or 23 percent, while ERAs dropped almost a full run, from 3.69 to 2.78. In 1901, Nap Lajoie of the Philadelphia Athletics hit .426—still the highest in A.L. history—and added 14 homers and 125 RBIs for the Triple Crown. Two years later, he led the league with a .344 mark.

Home runs all but disappeared from offenses, and were replaced by little-ball strategies including stolen bases, bunts, Baltimore chops and hit-and-runs. The 1902 Pittsburgh Pirates won the National League pennant with only 18 home runs. The 1906 Chicago White Sox were American League champions despite a .230 batting average and just seven homers, then pulled a World Series upset of the cross-town Chicago Cubs, who had won 116 games. No wonder those White Sox were called, "The Hitless Wonders."

Pittsburgh's Tommy Leach led the National League with six homers in 1902—none of which cleared a fence. Leach, all of 5-6 and 150 pounds, later said: "The fields were big then, and if you hit a ball between the outfielders and you were fast enough, you had a home run." Brooklyn's Jimmy Sheckard led with nine in 1903, the same number as league leader Harry Lumley of Brooklyn hit in 1904.

Philadelphia A's first baseman Frank "Home Run" Baker actually hit only 96 in his career but stole 235 bases. The tag came from two big homers he hit in the 1911 World Series, which followed a season in which he led the American League with 11 homers. In winning four consecutive home run titles, Baker hit all of 42 homers. Ty Cobb, the era's greatest hitter along with Honus Wagner, won the Triple Crown in 1909 with a .377 batting average but only nine homers and 109 RBI.

His prickly personality may have earned Gavvy Cravath the nickname 'Cactus', but nobody won more home run titles (6) in the Deadball Era.

Nobody fit the era's definition of a slugger any better than Cobb's longtime teammate, Sam Crawford. From 1899 to 1917, "Wahoo Sam" hit only 97 home runs—twice leading the league and once reaching double figures with 16. When he retired, he held the A.L. career record with 70 homers. But also among his 2,961 hits were 458 doubles and a record 309

triples. Throw in 366 stolen bases, and the profile of a Deadball Era cleanup hitter is complete. By comparison, Willie Mays, the greatest player of his era, belted 660 homers and 140 triples over a 22-year career that spanned 1951-73.

"The game is all different now; all power and lively balls and short fences and home runs," Crawford said almost 50 years after his career ended. "Back then, it was strategy and quick

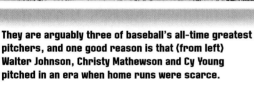

They are arguably three of baseball's all-time greatest pitchers, and one good reason is that (from left) Walter Johnson, Christy Mathewson and Cy Young pitched in an era when home runs were scarce.

thinking, and if you didn't play with your old noodle, you didn't play at all."

For a pure slugger, Cliff "Gavvy" Cravath is an unknown, but nobody won more home run titles (six) in the Deadball Era, and only Babe Ruth, Mike Schmidt and Ralph Kiner won more in their careers. Never heard of Gavvy? Because of his testy demeanor, he also was known as "Cactus". He belted 19 homers in 1913, when he also won the RBI title with 128, 33 more than the league runnerup, and five more home run championships in the next six years. His high was 24 in 1915, the most in the 1900s prior to 1919.

It's no coincidence three of the game's greatest pitchers of all-time—Cy Young, Christy Mathewson and Walter Johnson—flourished in the Deadball Era. Young wasn't so much a fireballer as he was a control artist and the leading example of pitchers' durability and longevity in the era. On his way to now-unthinkable career totals of 511 wins, 316 losses, 7,356 innings, a 2.63 ERA and 749 complete games in 906 starts, he led the league in wins five times, in complete games three times and in ERA and innings twice. He already was halfway through his career when the Deadball Era began, but added 225 wins onto his total after jumping from the National League to the new American League in 1901.

Mathewson won 30-plus games three consecutive years from 1903-05, and a career-high 37 games in 1908, when he also led the league with 34 complete games, 391 innings, 11 shutouts and a 1.43 ERA. With a 373-188 record from 1901-16, his career ERA was 2.13.

Johnson led the league in strikeouts 12 times in a 15-year span from 1910-24, pitched as many as 370 innings in three different seasons, and won 417 games while posting a 2.17 career ERA in 21 seasons. His 110 shutouts are a record, and in 65 of his losses, his Washington Senators were shut out. Even the often-acrimonious Cobb was impressed by Johnson's heater. "I watched him take that easy windup, and then something went past me that made me flinch," he said. "The thing just hissed with danger."

But that trio of legends had plenty of company when it came to mind-boggling accomplishments on the mound in the era. "Iron Man" Joe McGinnity threw 434 innings for the 1903 New York Giants, and pitched two games in the same day on five different occasions. "Happy Jack" Chesbro of the New York Highlanders won 41 of 51 starts and threw 48 complete games the following season. Boston's Smoky Joe Wood won 34 in 1912, 16 in a row and 10 by shutouts. In 1908, White Sox spitballer Ed Walsh set a record by pitching 464 innings while going 40-15 with a 1.42 ERA.

The 1907 World Series-champion Chicago

Cubs won 107 games and had five starters with at least 15 wins, all with ERAs below 1.70. No American League ERA leader in the 1900-10 decade had an ERA above 1.91 and only three N.L. leaders did. N.L. 1906 leader Mordecai "Three Finger" Brown posted a microscopic 1.04 ERA. When Cleveland's Addie Joss was perfect in a 1-0 victory over the White Sox on October 2, 1908, he had to be, as Walsh allowed an unearned run and four hits while striking out 15. The Phillies' Pete Alexander threw a record 16 shutouts in 1916, when he was 33-12 with 38 complete games and a 1.55 ERA. Between 1910 and 1920, 30 or more games were won in a season eight times—three times by Alexander. Since then, only Denny McLain has done it.

Doctoring the baseball was rampant—and entirely legal—until after the 1920 season, when 17 pitchers recognized as spitballers were grandfathered in, but nobody else was allowed to tamper with the baseball. Boston's staff of 1906-07 had so many pitchers doctoring the baseball that shortstop Al Bridwell later complained, "I had a devil of a time throwing the ball on a straight line from short to first base. The darn thing was always loaded."

The bottoming out for offenses came in 1908. Both leagues had measly .239 batting averages, and runs per game reached a decade low of 6.7 per game in the N.L. and 6.9 per game in the A.L. Seven no-hitters were thrown, and seven of the 50 all-time lowest single-season ERAs were posted that year.

A cork-center baseball known as the jack-rabbit ball was introduced in 1910 and used

For one season in 1912, there was nobody better with a bat than Cubs infielder Heinie Zimmerman.

He wasn't known as a home run hitter, but Ty Cobb always said he could hit them if he wanted to. He dominated all hitters from 1907 to 1919, a period in which he won 12-of-13 batting titles.

regularly in 1911, helping offenses gain back some of their muscle. Batting averages jumped to .260 in the N.L. and .273 in the A.L. in 1911, and runs bumped up to 8.8 per game and 9.2 per game, respectively. But it would take another decade, during which enclosed ballparks with more-reachable fences came into vogue, for the balance

of power to shift back to the hitters.

In the meantime, it was more of the same. And that meant hitting heroes named Cobb, Wagner, Speaker, Crawford, Baker and Zimmerman. Zimmerman? Yes, for one season (1912), there was nobody better in the National League than Cubs infielder Heinie Zimmerman, who is

Like Cobb, Honus Wagner was a dominant hitter of the Deadball Era who didn't need to use the home run as his primary weapon. In his 21-year career, he won six slugging percentage titles and finished in the top three in homers twice.

credited with winning a Triple Crown (there are discrepancies over his RBI total) with a .372 average, 14 homers and 103 RBIs. He would win two more RBI titles in a 13-year career, but never hit higher than .313 or reach double figures in homers again.

No, they don't fit the modern definition of sluggers, but to leave out Cobb and Wagner in a discussion of the era's sluggers would be criminal. The last of Wagner's eight batting titles in a 12-year span came in 1912. He never hit below .320 in that span, six times topping .350. While his home-run total was only 101 in a 21-year career, Wagner won six slugging percentage titles, finished in the top three in the league in homers two times, led the league in triples three times and doubles seven times, including four years in a row 1906-09.

Cobb's dominance stretched from 1907 to 1919, a period during which he won 10-of-13 batting titles, twice topped the .400 mark, batted .368 or above 11 years consecutive years, led the league in slugging percentage eight times, homers once, triples four times and doubles three times. In the 1911 season that first featured the cork-center ball, Cobb drove in 127 runs and had a .621 slugging percentage to go with a .420 batting average, 147 runs scored, 248 hits, 47 doubles and 24 triples.

And besides, Cobb said he could hit home runs if he wanted to, and proved it in 1925, when he changed his grip on the bat, altered his swing and hit five homers in two games before going back to his regular hitting style. That year he had his career high of 12 home runs.

By then, another change in the game led to a dramatic difference in how it was played between the white lines. As franchises stabilized and Sunday baseball became a cash cow, franchises began replacing old, wooden firetrap ballparks with concrete and steel structures. The first to take advantage of the new technology was Philadelphia A's owner Ben Shibe, whose name graced the park that opened in Philadelphia in 1909. Forbes Field also opened in Pittsburgh the same year, followed in the next few years by Comiskey Park (1910) and Wrigley Field (1916) in Chicago, Ebbets Field (1913) in Brooklyn, Navin Field (1912) in Detroit and Fenway Park (1912) in Boston.

Ben Shibe was the first owner who understood the importance of a ballpark to the team and the fans, erecting Shibe Park in Philadelphia in 1909 with its cavernous center field.

While Shibe's expanse included a 515-foot center field, the other parks were wedged into urban areas that forced smaller dimensions. For instance, long before the Green Monster, Fenway Park featured a steeply banked left field later dubbed Duffy's Cliff because left-fielder Duffy Lewis learned to play it well, topped a low wall just 320 feet from home plate.

It was in Boston in the late 1910s when the very nature of the game began to change again, as a very good lefthanded pitcher named George Herman "Babe" Ruth moved from the mound to the outfield to take advantage of the best power swing the game has ever known.

BABE
AND
THE REVOLUT

ION

Longtime Boston Red Sox star Harry Hooper says the idea was his. Near the end of a 12-year stay in Boston, Hooper, then the team captain, says he advised manager Ed Barrow to put Babe Ruth in the outfield on an everyday basis. No matter where the credit belongs, the bold yet logical move was the impetus that changed the game forever.

At that point in 1919, Ruth already was one of the American League's best pitchers. In four full seasons, he was 80-41, won 23 games and led the league in shutouts and ERA in 1916, and won 24 games and led the league by completing 35-of-41 starts in 1917. In addition, his postseason consecutive shutout innings streak reached 29, a record that stood for 42 years. But his bat was even better than his arm.

The transition actually began in 1918, when Ruth led the league in homers with 11 in only 95 games and 317 at-bats, while also going 13-7 with a 2.22 ERA in 20 games on the mound. In 1919, the switch became permanent, and Ruth's legend began in earnest. After that season, he made only five more pitching appearances.

Sportswriter Bob Broeg once wrote, "to try to capture Babe Ruth with cold statistics would be like trying to keep up with him on a night out." But we'll give it a whirl anyway: Twelve home run titles, including six in a row 1926-31; 13 slugging

Babe Ruth's Hall of Fame placard enshrines him in Cooperstown, but there are no plaques or trophies big enough to list all his accomplishments to the game.

percentage titles in a 14-year span; 10 on-base percentage titles including five at more than .500; eight times leading the league in runs scored; six RBI titles and 13 seasons of 100 or more; first all-time in at-bats to home runs, slugging percentage and walks; second all-time with 714 home runs, 2,213 RBIs, and 2,174 runs; a .342 career batting average, and 2,873 hits. He took over the all-time home run record in 1921, his third season as a fulltime hitter, and held it until 1974.

When Ruth led the league with 11 homers in 1918, the league hit only 96, with four teams totaling less than 10. He also out-homered four teams on his way to 29 in 1919, and put together arguably the most-dominant offensive season in history in 1920, when he hit more home runs than every other team in the league, won the title by 35 homers with 54, won the slugging percentage title by 215 points, led the league in RBIs, runs scored and on-base percentage, batted .376 and drew 51 more walks than any other player.

Ruth's 29 homers in 1919 marked the first time he set the single-season record, then he broke it two more years in succession with an incredible 54 in 1920 (his first year with the Yankees) and 59 in 1921. From 1926-31, he averaged better than 50 homers. The 60 homers he hit in 1927 stood as a record for 34 years, and

he lost a 13th home-run title because he missed the first six weeks of the 1922 season due to a suspension for participating in a prohibited barnstorming tour. Ruth's average season in the 1920s was a .355 batting average, 47 homers and 133 RBIs—not to mention six pennants and three World Series titles won by his Yankees. The "Sultan of Swat"? You bet.

Said teammate Sam Jones: "Babe Ruth could hit a ball so hard, and so far, that it was sometimes impossible to believe your eyes. We used to absolutely marvel at his hits. Tremendous wallops. You can't imagine the balls he hit. If Babe was as good relative to everybody else today as he used to be, he'd hit over 200 homers a season. That will give you an idea of how the big fellow dominated baseball back then."

Still, as monumental as Ruth's feats were, they weren't enough to alter the game on their own. Other factors contributed to Ruth's accomplishments and brought about the shift of dominance from the mound back to the batter's box. The start of the 1920s saw changes with major ramifications—the outlawing of the spitball and other "trick deliveries", and the use of far more new baseballs, which also were more lively due to a higher-grade woolen yarn that was wound tighter. Only 17 pitchers designated as spitballers were allowed to continue throwing the pitch, the last of whom (Burleigh Grimes) retired in 1934.

Ruth's hitting philosophy was, "I swing as hard as I can, and I try to swing right through the ball. I swing big, with everything I've got. I hit big or I miss big." Seeing the results—and Ruth's paychecks—other players began adopting it. The whiter, tighter baseball and shorter fences proved inviting to a new decade of sluggers, and little-ball strategies were pushed aside. Bats changed along with the philosophical shift, with thinner handles and bigger knobs accommodating hitters

who moved their hands down on the handle.

The 1920 season—the first with the new baseballs—produced dramatic offensive increases. The major-league home run total jumped 40 percent from 447 to 630, runs were up 24 percent from 8,657 to 10,762, batting averages from .258 to .270 in the National League and .268 to .284 in American League.

The 1920-25 seasons produced unmatched power and average numbers, including no less than seven .400 seasons – three by the Cardinals' Rogers Hornsby, two by the Browns' George Sisler, and one each by Tigers teammates Ty Cobb

The 1920-25 seasons produced unmatched power, as there were no less than seven .400 seasons—including three by the Cardinals' Rogers Hornsby (left) and one by the Tigers' Harry Heilmann (below).

and Harry Heilmann.

Hornsby won six consecutive batting titles in 1920-25, never hitting below .370, as well as six consecutive slugging percentage titles, and a Triple Crown in 1922 with a .401 average, 42 homers and 152 RBIs. In another of the great single-season offensive performances of all time, he also led the league in slugging percentage (.559), hits (250), doubles (46), total bases (450) and runs (141) that season. Hornsby's 1925 season was only a shade below, with another Triple Crown at .403, 39 homers, 143 RBIs and a National League record .756 slugging percentage.

Sisler stroked a record 257 hits in 1920. Heilmann, one of the game's most underrated hitters in history, won four batting titles in a seven-year span 1921-27 with averages of .394, .403, .393 and .398, and was only nine hits away from hitting .400 in all four of those seasons.

Even John McGraw, the master practitioner of the running game, conceded the obvious in 1923: "With the ball being hit all about the lot, the necessity of taking chances on the bases has decreased. ... There is no use in sending men down on a long chance of stealing a bag when there is a better chance of the batter hitting one

for two bases, or maybe, out of the lot."

By 1925, runs per game jumped back into double figures for the first time since the 1890s, at 10.1 in the National League and 10.4 in the American League. In all, 1,169 homers were hit that season, up 250 percent from 1917.

The 1927 season showcased arguably the game's greatest offensive team—the Murderer's Row Yankees. Ruth's 60 homers—No. 60 came on the final day of the season off Washington's Tom Zachary at Yankee Stadium—were 13 more than league runner-up Lou Gehrig, and double the total of National League co-leaders Hack Wilson and Cy Williams.

Ruth and Gehrig finished 1-2 in the majors in homers, runs, total bases, slugging percentage, RBIs and walks. Earle Combs led the league in hits and triples, and finished third in runs and total bases. Tony Lazzeri was third in the league in homers. The Bronx Bombers scored 975 runs, the rest of the league averaged 731. They belted 158 homers, no other A.L. team hit more than 56. Their slugging average was .489, only two other teams topped the .400 mark. All that slugging translated into a 110-44 record, a runaway American League championship by 19 games and a sweep of the Pittsburgh Pirates in the World Series.

The 1929 season was a landmark one for home runs in the National League, whose eight teams combined for 754 home runs. The previous high in the decade was 636 in 1925. The 754 figure was almost four times the National League total of 1919. Leading the way was a Philadelphia Phillies team that all but accounted for the increase by jumping from 85 homers in a 43-109 season in 1928 to a league-leading 153 homers while improving to 71-82 in 1929.

Like Ruth in Yankee Stadium, Chuck Klein's lefthanded power stroke was a perfect fit in Philadelphia's Baker Bowl, where the wall was only 280 feet away down the right-field line. That resulted in one of the greatest five-year power production runs, as Klein won four home run titles, three slugging percentage titles and two RBI titles, led the league in runs three times and hits twice, and won a Triple Crown in 1933 with a .368 average, 28 homers and 120 RBIs. That same season, Jimmie Foxx won an American League Triple Crown for the Philadelphia Athletics, marking the only double Triple Crown season.

Ironically, Klein's best season numbers-wise earned him no individual titles. That came in 1930, the greatest offensive season on record. Concerned about possible attendance decline due to the onset of the Depression, the National League livened up the ball again, and lowered the height of the stitching. The results were eye-opening. The league hit .303, with six of eight teams topping .300 led by the New York Giants at .319. Runs jumped to 11.4 per game in the National League, and five teams hit more than 100 homers led by the Chicago Cubs with 171.

Fifty-six of those came off the bat of Hack Wilson, a squat, barrel-chested slugger with a size 18 neck and size six shoes—the first real challenge of Ruth's home run record. While that National League record total would stand for 68 years, it wasn't Wilson's biggest accomplishment in a season of monumental numbers, as he also drove in a major-league record 190 runs. Klein exploded for a .386 average, 40 homers, 170 RBIs and 250 hits, but only finished third in the batting race and second in the other three categories. The Giants' Bill Terry became the eighth player to hit

Lou Gehrig (left) and the Babe were the two biggest catalysts for arguably the game's greatest offensive team—the 1927 Yankees. In that year, Ruth and Gehrig finished 1-2 in the majors in homers, runs, total bases, slugging percentage, RBIs and walks.

Three top sluggers of the 1930s were Mel Ott (right) who won five home run titles in the decade; Jimmie Foxx (below, top) who hit 58 homers in 1932; and Chuck Klein (below, bottom) who won home run titles in 1931 and 1933.

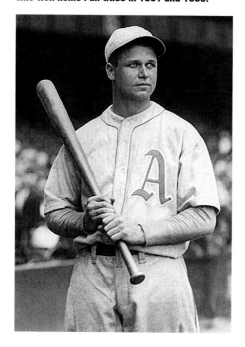

.400 since 1920, finishing at .401 with 254 hits. The American League was hardly a collective slouch, hitting .288 with 673 home runs.

But the offensive bubble burst a bit along with the nation's economy, and the game suffered at the gate and on the field in the first half of the 1930s. As Ruth and other sluggers from the 1920s began to fade (he last led the league in homers in 1931, and his "called-shot" World Series homer in 1932 was his last in the postseason), there were no immediate replacements, particularly in the National League. By 1933, runs were down from 11.4 per game in the National League in 1930 to 7.9 in 1933.

Klein won National League home run titles with

only 31 in 1931 and 28 in 1933. Mel Ott won five home run titles and finished no worse than third each year from 1931 to 1939 yet averaged 31.4 homers during that span. Again, it was the case of a lefthanded swing tailored to a very short right-field porch, as Ott hit 323 of his 511 career home runs in his home park, the Polo Grounds, where the fence was just 257 feet down the right-field line. He would become the National League's first 500-homer man in 1945.

The American League's offensive numbers held up through the 1930s thanks to the presence of four of the game's all-time greatest sluggers—Gehrig, Foxx, Hank Greenberg, and beginning in 1936, Joe DiMaggio. In fact, the A.L. in the 1930s saw two of the top eight stretches of individual home run hitting: Foxx belted 241 in his five best seasons from 1932-39 (58, 50, 48, 44, 41)—good enough for third all-time behind Mark McGwire (294) and Ruth (276)—and Gehrig totaled 232 (49, 49, 47, 46, 41) in his five top seasons.

All 10 players with the highest RBI totals in their five best years—Gehrig, Foxx, Ruth, Greenberg, Simmons, Wilson, DiMaggio, Hornsby, Williams, Klein—played in the '30s, and most did the most damage in the decade. Here's what it took to lead the A.L. in RBIs: 1930: Gehrig (174), 1931: Gehrig (184), 1932: Foxx (169), 1933: Foxx (163), 1934: Gehrig (165), 1935: Greenberg (170), 1936: Hal Trosky (162), 1937: Greenberg (183), 1938: Foxx (175) and 1939: Ted Williams (145).

In 1932, the menacing and powerful Foxx fell just two homers short of Ruth's total of 60. Three times, Foxx topped the .700 mark in slugging percentage, including a .749 mark in 1932, the highest since Ruth's remarkable .772 in 1927. In 1938, Foxx hit 50 homers and won the RBI crown

The Cubs' Hack Wilson set the National League gold standard with 56 home runs and 190 RBIs in 1930. The home run record stood for 68 years; the RBI record still stands.

by 29 with 175, the batting title with a .349 mark and the slugging percentage title with a .704 mark.

The term "bat speed" wouldn't gain credibility until nearly 60 years later, but Foxx became one of its first and foremost practitioners, mightily swinging a 37-ounce bat through the strike zone with his huge biceps and forearms. In 1940, he became the youngest player to reach 500 homers, at age 33.

Pitcher Lefty Grove said about Foxx, "he wasn't scouted, he was trapped." And sportswriter Red Smith once described one of Foxx's blasts at Shibe Park this way: "It looked like a low line drive streaking over the infield, but it was still climbing when it clipped the very peak of the roofed upper deck in left and took off for the clouds. Three days later, a small boy in Bustleton, on the northeast fringe of town, found a baseball with snow on it."

Greenberg's run at Ruth's record came in 1938, when he had 46 homers on September 1 and 58 with five games to play, but didn't hit another in the final five games. And in 1939, a lanky lefthanded hitter burst onto the scene by leading the league in RBIs with 145 and total bases with 344. If there were a Rookie of the Year award back then, Ted Williams would have won it in a landslide, as he also finished second in the league in runs, doubles and walks.

Greenberg would win another home run title in 1940, then Williams dominated the two World War II seasons, winning back-to-back batting and home run titles, and one RBI title, missing two consecutive Triple Crowns by only five RBIs in 1941, when DiMaggio won that race with 125. In

Detroit's Hank Greenberg was a feared hitter of the 1930s and '40s, and very nearly broke Ruth's home run record in 1938 when he finished with 58 homers.

53, when he served in the Korean War. Considering that in his 17 full seasons, Williams averaged 30 homers, 106 RBIs and 154 hits, with five more similar years onto his totals, he could have had an estimated 671 homers (3rd all-time), 2,332 RBIs (1st all-time) and 3,383 hits (8th all-time).

DiMaggio also missed the entire 1943-45 seasons, likely costing him anywhere from 80-100 homers and 375-400 RBIs. Put those onto his career totals, and he would have hit about 450 homers and driven in about 1,900 runs to go with a .325 batting average. Greenberg and Johnny Mize also lost serious numbers off their career totals due to military service. In between home run and RBI titles in 1940 and 1946, Greenberg lost 4-plus seasons, leaving his relatively modest career totals at 331 homers and 1,276 RBIs. Estimating his lost production at 180 homers and 585 RBIs (40 homers and 130 RBIs), his career totals would have

1941-42, Williams hit 73 homers, drove in 257 runs and batted .379 (.406 and .356).

No slugger would be hurt more by the war years than Williams, who lost not only the 1943-45 seasons following his near back-to-back Triple Crowns, but also almost two full seasons in 1952-

jumped to 511 homers and 1,861 RBIs. Mize's three lost seasons cost him the chance to go over 400 homers and 1,600 RBIs.

A list of sluggers in the era between the two World Wars wouldn't be complete without Negro League legends Josh Gibson and Buck Leonard.

Josh Gibson (left) and Buck Leonard (above, hitting) were two of the top sluggers of the Negro Leagues and often are compared to Ruth and Gehrig, as the two men batted back-to-back in the lineup for the Homestead Grays and led the team to nine titles.

What could they have done in a major-league setting? We'll never know, but their place in the Hall of Fame should be assurance that they would have been superstars in any league.

Gibson widely is compared to Ruth. In 13 full seasons, he won 10 Negro League home run titles and four batting titles. His career average of .384 is the highest in Negro League history, and he reportedly hit as many as 84 homers in a year. Gibson also hit them as far as anybody. A home run at Yankee Stadium hit near the top of the wall behind the centerfield bleachers, an estimate 580 feet. Another reportedly went over the third deck in left field, the only fair ball ever hit out of that

stadium. Sadly and ironically, Gibson died of a cerebral hemorrhage at age 35 in 1947, a few months before Jackie Robinson broke baseball's color barrier.

If Gibson was the Babe Ruth of the Negro Leagues, then first baseman Buck Leonard was Lou Gehrig. The two batted back-to-back in the Homestead Grays lineup, Gibson's righthanded power followed by Leonard's lefthanded dead-pull hitting stroke, leading the Grays to nine consecutive Negro National League titles from 1937 to 1945. Leonard was 39 when Robinson broke in with Brooklyn, and thought he was too far past his prime to play in the big leagues.

RBUST

Mickey Mantle,
New York Yankees

It was a different

brand of major-league baseball played in the 1943-45 period interrupted by World War II, and slugging certainly suffered as a result. With most of the game's stars overseas and economic restrictions in place in the United States, the game was a shell of itself. Even the ball was altered, as a rubber shortage forced use of a ball that didn't travel as far.

The Cubs' Bill "Swish" Nicholson and Detroit's Rudy York were the only two legitimate sluggers in their prime who remained on big-league rosters, and they won three home run titles between them in 1943-44. Stan Musial, the National League batting champion in his second full season in 1943, hadn't yet developed his power stroke. Mel Ott was past his prime and young Vern Stephens was just coming into his own with the St. Louis Browns before some bigger years in Boston. Pitching was suspect enough that Boston's Tommy Holmes, who hit only 88 homers in an 11-year career that spanned 1942-52, belted 13 of those in 1944 and a league-leading 28 in 1945.

But with the return of the game's big bashers in 1946, power production returned for a long sustained climb that would last into the early 1960s. In the stable, pre-expansion, 154-game-seasons after the end of the war, offenses shifted into a big power/low batting average mode that led to unprecedented home run totals but only modest run totals.

League batting averages settled into the .253-.266 range, and stuck there. From 1947-1960, only once did either league vary from that mode, as the American League batted .271 in 1950. Nobody had more than 37 stolen bases from 1947-55, and when Willie Mays stole 40 in 1956, he all but

The 1940s really were the days of sitting back and waiting for the three-run homer, as big, slow-footed sluggers like Ted Kluszewski (right) dotted rosters everywhere.

In the years after World War II, there was no better slugger than Pittsburgh's Ralph Kiner (above, and at left, being congratulated by his teammates for yet another home run.)

doubled up A.L. stolen-base leader Luis Aparicio's total of 21. Jackie Robinson won the National League stolen base title with 29 in his 1947 breakthrough season, and nobody else in the league stole more than 14. Sam Jethroe's 35 steals led the National League in 1950, more than doubling runner-up Pee Wee Reese's 17, and Dom DiMaggio led the American League with only 15 that season.

Yes, these really were the days of sitting back and waiting for the three-run homer, a philosophy later espoused by Orioles manager

Earl Weaver in his successful run that began in 1969. Big, slow-footed sluggers dotted rosters everywhere—Walt Dropo, Gus Zernial and Ted Kluszewski to name three. In 1947, when Johnny Mize and Ralph Kiner tied for the league lead with 51 homers, 886 were hit in the National League, only six fewer than in the monumental slugging year of 1930. However, only 5,666 runs were scored compared to 7,025 in 1930, when the National League hit a combined .303, 38 points higher than in 1947.

By 1950, teams hitting 100 or more home runs were the norm, and the National League topped the 1,000 mark for the first time in history with exactly 1,100, led by Brooklyn's 194. The American League wasn't far behind with 973, although Cleveland's Al Rosen led the league with only 37. The National League topped 1,000 homers every year between 1950 and 1961 with the exception of 1952 (907), and averaged just under 1,200 per season from 1954-59. The

American League began a similar stretch in 1956, averaging 1,067 through 1960.

In an era filled with them, there was no better slugger in the years after World War II than Kiner. Although his Pirates team was a perennial also-ran behind the Dodgers and Giants, Kiner won or shared seven consecutive National League home run titles—a string not even Ruth attained. His seven crowns trail only Ruth (12) and Mike Schmidt (8), and his ratio of at-bats to homers is exceeded only by Ruth and Mark McGwire. The string of titles came in Kiner's first seven seasons in the league—1946-52—with totals of 23, 51, 40, 54, 47, 42 and 37 homers. How dominant was Kiner in those years? He hit 294 homers during his seven-year reign, an average of 42 per year.

Before the 1947 season, the Pirates obtained another legendary righthanded slugger—Hank Greenberg—and tailored Forbes Field for the powerful duo. A double bullpen was constructed that cut the left-field wall to 335 feet away down the line and 355 feet in the power alley, forming "Greenberg Gardens" which later became "Kiner's Korner".

Sooner or later, any discussion of 1950 major league baseball has to turn to New York City. The three teams there won all but two pennants from 1950-57. The Yankees took all but two pennants in the decade—1954 and 1959. Between the Phillies' Whiz Kids pennant in 1950 and the

Milwaukee Braves' title in 1957, the Dodgers won four times and the Giants twice before heading west.

Three of the big reasons were slugging center fielders Mickey Mantle, Willie Mays and Duke Snider. Mantle and Mays would be linked with Hank Aaron throughout the next two decades, as they built numbers that put them among the greatest sluggers of all time. But in the Big Apple in the 1950s, they dueled with Snider for center field supremacy. What all four of those sluggers brought were speed, grace, athleticism and defense that stood out in an era of plodding, one-dimensional players, forever changing the image of a superstar.

Mantle and Mays both arrived in 1951, and became dominant by 1954. Mantle hit .300 with 27 homers, 102 RBIs and a league-leading 129 runs scored in 1954, won home run and slugging percentage titles in 1955 and the 1956 Triple Crown with a .353 average, 52 homers and 130 RBIs in his career year. Between 1955 and 1962, Mantle won one batting title, one RBI title, four home run titles and four slugging titles.

Mays came back from almost two years of military service and exploded for 41 homers, 110 RBIs and a league-leading .345 batting average in 1954. He won the home-run title the next season with 51 (one of his two 50-homer seasons) and also led the league in slugging percentage and triples in 1954, 1955 and 1957.

Snider was more consistently excellent if not spectacular, hitting between 40-43 homers and driving in between 92 and 136 RBIs the last five seasons in Brooklyn.

It was during the 1954 season—the Braves' first in Milwaukee—that Aaron, a rookie infielder, was tried in left field after Bobby Thomson broke his ankle. Aaron responded with 13 homers and 69 RBIs in 122 games, and wouldn't hit fewer

Three reasons the 1950s exploded with power—and the Dodgers and Giants dominated the National League—were because of (clockwise) Willie Mays, Duke Snider and Mickey Mantle.

than 24 in any season until 20 years later, when he belted an Al Downing pitch into history, passing Babe Ruth as the game's all-time home run leader.

Aaron would never put together a 50-homer season, but he would top 40 eight times including a career-high 47 in 1971, win four home run titles and four RBI titles, and belt more homers after his 30th birthday (413) than before (342).

But Mays, Mantle, Aaron and Snider hardly were the only sluggers to emerge in the 1950s. In fact, other than the 1990s, no decade saw the infusion of more raw power and slugging legends.

With Jackie Robinson already having paved the way, black talent trickled onto big-league rosters throughout the 1950s. Ernie Banks made his debut with the Cubs in 1953, beginning a 19-year run that would see him hit 512 home runs, including a string of 40 or more in five of six seasons 1955-60— unheard of for a shortstop at that time.

Frank Robinson brought an unrelenting competitiveness along with a powerful stroke that made an immediate impact on the National League in 1956, when he was voted Rookie of the

Year after hitting .290 with 38 homers and 83 RBIs. There would be only one batting title, one home run title and one RBI title in his 21 seasons—all coming in his Triple Crown season of 1966—but Robinson would total 586 home runs and 1,812 RBIs. Only Aaron, Ruth and Mays have hit more homers, and only 14 players drove in more runs.

Other than the 1990s, no decade saw an infusion of power more than the 1950s because of these four sluggers, each of whom would hit more than 500 homers in their careers. Sluggers such as Hank Aaron (left), baseball's home run king; Frank Robinson (above left), Harmon Killebrew (above right) and Eddie Mathews.

Three more of the game's top dozen sluggers, and another whose name would sit atop the single-season home run list longer than any other player including Ruth, made their debuts in the 1950s, although they wouldn't make their marks until the 1960s.

Harmon Killebrew came out of Idaho as a bonus baby at age 18 and shuttled between the minors and the Washington Senators' bench for five seasons. When his chance came, he made the most of it, hitting 380 homers the season he turned 31 and 476 the season he turned 34, prompting speculation that he had a shot at Ruth's 714. Along the way came a shot entirely out of Tiger Stadium (one of only four to

clear the left-field roof), and a 530-foot blast into the upper deck at Minnesota's Metropolitan Stadium that shattered two seats. "Killer" averaged 39 homers from 1959-70, topped 40 eight times and won six home run titles, including three in a row in 1962-64 with totals of 48, 45 and 49. But after his final 40-homer season in 1970, Killebrew topped 25 just two more times, and hit only 32 over his final three seasons to finish with 573.

Willie McCovey played only 52 games in his first season, but his .354 average and 13 homers were enough to win him the 1959 National League Rookie of the Year award. He won his first home run title in 1963, and would

Mickey Mantle and Roger Maris powered the Yankees of the 1950s, and in 1961, Maris wrote himself into baseball immortality by breaking Babe Ruth's then-single season home run record.

add two more in 1968 and 1969, when he also won RBI and slugging percentage titles. On his way to 521 career homers, he was the first of only two players to hit two homers in an inning on two occasions (Jeff King was the other).

Eddie Mathews was yet another 500-homer man whose career spanned the 1950s and 1960s. He broke in just in time for the Braves' final season in Boston in 1952, and stayed in a Braves uniform for two franchise moves through 1966. His two home run titles came in Milwaukee in 1953 and 1959.

By 1961, not only had the Giants, Dodgers, Braves, Athletics and Browns relocated, but the game's increasing popularity nationwide led to American League expansion into Minnesota and Los Angeles. The National League would follow a year later, getting back into New York with the Mets, and adding the Houston Colt .45s.

With the additional teams came the increase to a 162-game schedule, giving commissioner Ford Frick reason to threaten to put an asterisk next to

Roger Maris' name when he one-upped Ruth with 61 homers in 1961. And that was only the beginning of the unfortunate opposition and derision aimed at Maris. Media scrutiny and death threats unnerved him enough that he withdrew, and lost some of his hair.

After 141 games, Maris was only five short of Ruth's record, but a seven-game drought cut into his chase. Number 60 came in the Yankees' 159th game of the season off Baltimore's Jack Fisher in Yankee Stadium, and the record-breaker came in the 163rd and final game, off Boston's Tracy Stallard, also in Yankee Stadium.

Popular sentiment was that a dilution of pitching contributed heavily to Maris' one-upping Ruth. After a career year in '61 in which he won the batting title with a .361 mark to go with 41 homers and 132 RBIs, Detroit first baseman Norm Cash even joked, "I owe my success to expansion pitching, a short right-field fence and my hollow bats."

But in truth, the numbers weren't significantly different in the American League from 1960 to 1961, and the effects of expansion really wouldn't be felt until another round at the end of the decade, when other changes were made to boost offense. The American League batting average climbed only one point to .256 in 1961. Home runs in both leagues increased only from 1.76 in 1960 to 1.93 per game in 1961, and runs from 8.62 per game to 9.05.

Although the 1960s weren't really known as a slugger's decade, Boston's Carl Yastrzemski won a Triple Crown in 1967 with a .326 average, 121 RBIs and 44 homers.

Not everybody bought into the idea that slugging had become an easier proposition than it had been in the past. As Maris and Mantle took sights on Ruth during the 1961 season in which they combined to hit 115 homers, Greenberg, then a front-office executive, said: "What I've grown to resent is a great inclination on the part of many to deprecate the feat even before it is accomplished. They speak of the lively ball, expansion, dilution of pitching, smaller ballparks and all that nonsense. As much as I revered the Babe, I still feel that he was not subjected to the strains of day and night baseball, the constant travel and the frantic publicity commotion that has to be unsettling to these two young men. I'm convinced that the accomplishment of breaking the record is greater now than it ever was."

But it would take until 37 years later for Maris to get his just due, as his memory and surviving family members were made a part of the record-breaking run by Mark McGwire and Sammy Sosa in 1998.

The rest of the 1960s quickly degenerated into a slugging morass reminiscent of the game's first two decades in the 20th century, as a generation of exceptional pitchers took control of the game and strangled the offense out of it. That should have brought about a greater sense of acknowledgment of Maris' feat, but it never materialized. Instead, Maris' quick decline as a power hitter prompted a one-year wonder sentiment to grow.

Home runs and runs per game actually decreased with the National League expansion of 1962, dropping from 1.93 homers per game to 1.78, and 9.05 runs per game to 8.96. Another drop occurred in 1963, and the bottoming out came in the great pitching year of 1968, when teams hit just 1.20 homers per game and scored only 6.83 runs per game. The American League followed a remarkably similar decline through 1968, when runs were down to 6.8 per game and homers were at 1.4 per game. Even baseball's All-Star Game, where the greatest collection of sluggers gather each July, suffered. The 1967 game was a mind-numbing 2-1 affair that took 15 innings to decide. The following year, the National League won 1-0.

Two factors in the offensive decline was an expanded strike zone beginning in 1963, when it was stretched from the top of the shoulders to the bottom of the knees, and more liberal use of hard-throwing relief pitchers.

There still were great slugging

accomplishments in the decade—Triple Crowns by Robinson in 1966 and Boston's Carl Yastrzemski in 1967; Mays' 52 homers in 1965, capping a run of three home run titles in four years, Killebrew's three consecutive home-run titles and four consecutive seasons of 40-plus, and gargantuan Frank Howard belting 136 homers in a three-year span, winning home run titles in 1968 and 1970.

But for the most part, it was a forgettable time for sluggers. Boston's Tony Conigliaro led the A.L. with only 32 homers in 1965, Yastrzemski won a batting title with a measly .301 mark in 1968, when he was the only A.L. player to hit higher than .290. Three-hundred hitters were particularly scarce in the American League, which had only 19 in the 1963-68 seasons. League batting averages were scarily low, dipping into the .240s in 1963, and as low as .236 in the American League in 1967 and .230 in 1968, when only six major-leaguers topped the .300 mark. The World Series champion Tigers got there despite an infield that hit a combined .229.

And of course, the pitching accomplishments were mind-boggling. Arguably, there never has been a better stretch of pitching than that of Sandy Koufax from 1961-66. He was 129-47, led the league in ERA five times, strikeouts four times, in wins and shutouts three times, complete games twice with 27 each time, threw 35 shutouts, won three Cy Young Awards and pitched four no-hitters. The pitching numbers from 1968 finally convinced the game's leaders that something had to be done. Denny McLain won 31 games and his 1.96 ERA was good enough only for fourth place. Bob Gibson's ERA was 1.12—the lowest since 1914—and he still lost nine games while winning 22. Don Drysdale threw six consecutive shutouts and a then-record 58⅔ consecutive scoreless innings, and both league's ERAs dipped just below 3.00 at 2.99 in the National and 2.98 in the American.

CHANGI

Ken Griffey Jr.,
Seattle Mariners

TIMES

NG

Times, they were

a changin' socially in the 1960s, and by 1969, the same was true in the national pastime. The mound was lowered from 15 inches to 10, the strike zone was reduced to include only the armpits to the top of the knees, and another round of expansion brought four new franchises in Kansas City, Seattle, Montreal and San Diego and a four-division six-team format. As a result, offensive numbers went boom, beginning a lengthy climb that reached unprecedented heights in the latter half of the 1990s. And following the historic pattern, attendance climbed with offense, jumping by nearly 50 percent from 1969 to 1979.

The theory that expansion dilutes pitching? It gained its momentum with this round of

Thanks to league expansion, Atlanta's Rico Carty (above) had the N.L.'s highest average in 22 years in 1970 with .366, and St. Louis' Joe Torre followed it up with .363 in 1971.

franchise additions. In 1969, offense increased more than a run per game (to 8.1 in the N.L. and 8.2 in the A.L.) and homers by one-half per game. The National League had a similar increase the following year, and the league's batting average made its move up into the .250s in the first half of the 1970s. Atlanta's Rico Carty hit .366 in 1970—the league's highest average in 22 years— and St. Louis' Joe Torre hit .363 the following season.

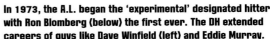
In 1973, the A.L. began the 'experimental' designated hitter with Ron Blomberg (below) the first ever. The DH extended careers of guys like Dave Winfield (left) and Eddie Murray.

But American League numbers lagged in 1971 and 1972, when the league batting average dropped back to .247 and then .239, prompting one of the modern generation's most controversial and divisive rule changes—the designated hitter. What began as an experiment remains in force today in the American League, and a generation of hitting accomplishments has been aided by it, as aging sluggers such as Dave Winfield, Eddie Murray and Dave Kingman had a place in the lineup to add to their lustrous career totals.

The Yankees' Ron Blomberg was the first designated hitter, but only because the Yankees-Red Sox game was the first to begin on opening day of the 1973 season. The Yankees scored two runs in the top of the first inning to bring Blomberg, the No. 6 hitter, to the plate before

Boston cleanup hitter and designated hitter Orlando Cepeda got a chance to hit.

American League run production jumped dramatically with the change—1.5 more runs per game—and 377 more homers were hit. Both leagues topped the 1,500-homer mark for the first time in 1973, an average of 1.6 per game, as another generation of sluggers came into its own. The 1973 season also marked the first time a team had three players hit 40 or more home runs, as Atlanta's Aaron (40), Darrell Evans (41) and Davey Johnson (43) turned the trick.

Cincinnati's Johnny Bench set slugging marks for catchers, winning home run and RBI titles in Most Valuable Player seasons in 1970 and 1972. He was the first catcher in the century to lead his league in homers, and one of only four to do so in RBIs.

Pittsburgh's Willie Stargell, a classic power hitter who earned the nickname "Pops" later in his Hall of Fame career, began a string of 13 consecutive 20-homer seasons in 1964 and averaged 30 homers a season from 1970-79. Along the way, he hit seven homers out of Forbes Field, and topped it off with league-leading totals of 48 in 1971 and 44 in 1973.

It was no coincidence that Stargell's biggest home run years came after the Pirates moved from Forbes Field, with its high screen above the right-field fence, to Three Rivers Stadium. He

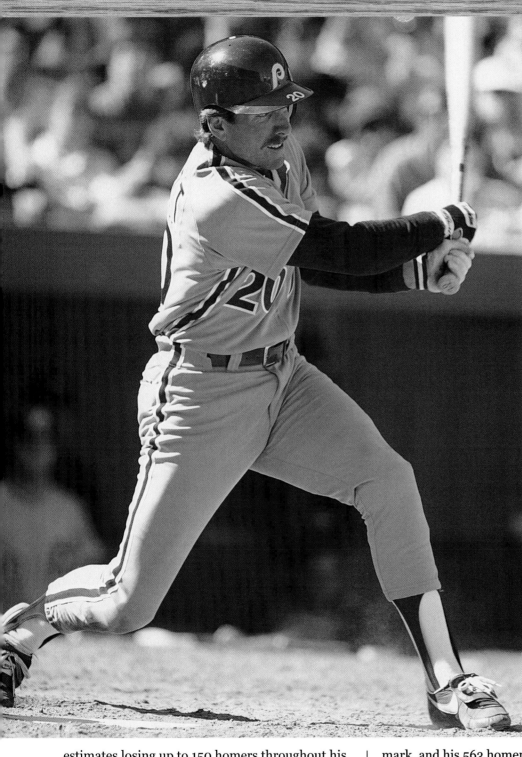

three in one game in the 1977 World Series, but exploded into stardom in his second full season in 1969, when he set career highs with 47 homers and 118 RBIs. Still, his totals were tainted by a sense of "what-could-have-been", as he had 40 homers by July 29th, then slumped terribly. The irrepressible and flamboyant Jackson would go on to win four home run titles, one Most Valuable Player award, and hit 30-plus homers six more times. Nobody has a better World Series slugging average than his .755

estimates losing up to 150 homers throughout his career at Forbes, costing him a place in the 600-homer club, as he finished with 475. Typical of the all-or-nothing style of sluggers that became prominent after World War II, Stargell trails only Reggie Jackson in career strikeouts.

Jackson later would earn the tag "Mr. October" for his 16 postseason homers including

mark, and his 563 homers remain sixth all-time.

Mike Schmidt's run of eight home-run titles began with three in succession 1974-76 before George Foster slugged 52 homers in 1977 to become the first National Leaguer in 12 years to reach the 50 mark. No American Leaguer hit as many as 40 homers between 1971-77, a period during which Jackson won two titles and finished

In 1977, Cincinnati's George Foster hit 52 homers to become the first National Leaguer in 12 years to reach the 50 mark. And Dick Allen (right) cashed in on his hitting prowess, earning a three-year $750,000 contract in 1973.

.266 in the American League. An amazing 518 more homers were hit in the National League in 1977 than in 1976, a 46 percent jump. Leading the way were the Dodgers, who established a major-league record with four players at 30 or more homers, Steve Garvey (33), Ron Cey (30), Dusty Baker (30) and Reggie Smith (32). The 1977 season also saw Hall of Famer Rod Carew hit .388—the highest average in the American League in 20 years—for one of his six batting titles in the decade.

Schmidt hit 45 homers in 1979 only to finish second to Dave Kingman, a lanky, laconic slugger with little else to his game. In one of the greatest slugfests in the game's history, those two combined for five homers in a 23-22 Philadelphia Phillies' victory over the Cubs on May 17, 1979. Kingman hit three tape-measure blasts onto Waveland Avenue beyond the left-field stands, while Schmidt hit the first and last homers in a game that featured 50 hits, 23 of them for extra bases and 11 home runs.

many as 40 homers between 1971-77, a period during which Jackson won two titles and finished second four times, and controversial slugger Dick Allen, who became the game's highest-paid player when he signed a three-year $750,000 contract in 1973, won two titles. Within a decade, Allen's salary would become merely average, as the era of free agency was ushered in during the 1976 season.

Offenses got another boost when the American League expanded again in 1977, when Seattle and Toronto entered the league. From 1976 to 1977, runs jumped by one per game and the league batting average climbed from .256 to

Schmidt would win six of the first seven National League home-run titles in the 1980s, as he belted a career-high 48 in 1980 and 31 in 102 games in the strike-shortened 1981 season. Kingman's other title came in 1982, and he would go onto to the ignominious distinction of being the player with the most career home runs (442) who isn't in the Hall of Fame.

But Kingman was more the exception than the rule in the 1980s, as artificial turf surfaces brought about a renewed emphasis on hitting for average and the use of speed. Beginning with the Astrodome in 1964, the National League in particular became turf-infested, with half its 12 teams playing home games on it. The American League had it in only four of 14 parks.

George Brett provided power and charm in Kansas City, and his flirtation with .400 in 1980 (he finished with .390) was one of the decade's biggest power stories.

It's not that power numbers suffered much. But the decade's biggest offensive accomplishments were George Brett flirting with .400 and finishing at .390 in 1980, Rickey Henderson stealing 130 bases in 1982 and Pete Rose breaking Ty Cobb's all-time hit record on September 11, 1985. One alarming trend was a rise in strikeouts in both leagues. Strikeouts rose about 20 percent in both leagues between 1980 to 1986, and peaked in the American League in 1987 at 11.8 per game.

Curiously, league home run totals skyrocketed that season, and despite league officials' denials, many believe balls were juiced, as players who never before or since displayed surprising power. In all, a record 4,458 homers were hit, up 17 percent. Wade Boggs, who would reach the 3,000-hit mark 12 years later, belted 24 homers

in 1987, but had only one other season in double figures in his 18-year career. Wally Joyner hit 34, and never had another season above 21 after that. Rookie Matt Nokes broke in with a bang with 32 homers, but had only two more seasons above 20. But one genuine slugger—arguably the greatest of all-time—first made his mark that season by leading the American League with 49 homers. Eleven seasons later, Mark McGwire would go 21 better, and stand alone at the new milestone of 70 homers.

It was McGwire's teammate in Oakland—Jose Canseco—who ushered in the latest trend in the game with a breakthrough 40-homer, 40-steal season in 1988. Never before had one player combined so much power, muscle and speed. Nor had one used a weight-training regimen to such success. At 6-4, 240 pounds, he was bigger than

Babe Ruth, yet faster than Ty Cobb. Bigger became better. Weight-lifting regimens that used to be shunned by big leaguers because of the fear of losing flexibility became commonplace. Bat speed was even more in vogue, as a new generation of muscular yet sleek sluggers were whipping thin-handled bats in the 32-34-ounce range through the strike zone. And in general, players were just bigger than the generations that preceded them. Consider: Harmon Killebrew, who only a generation ago was known as "Killer" because of his bulk and home run prowess, was only 5-11 and 215 pounds. Jimmie Foxx, known as "The Beast", was 6-0, 195, about average size for a player in the 1990s.

Cecil Fielder didn't exactly fit that sleek and muscular description, but there was no better slugger in the game in the early 1990s. "Big Daddy" burst back onto the big-league scene after a season in Japan, hitting a major-league-leading 51 homers in 1990 for Detroit to become the 12th player to reach the 50 mark and first in the American League since 1961. Fielder, whose weight eventually would balloon to about 300

Cecil Fielder was neither sleek, speedy or muscular, but he was the definitive slugger of the early 1990s.

The Bash Brothers, Mark McGwire and Jose Canseco, ushered in a new breed of power hitter—a combination of power, muscle and speed.

pounds, won another home run title in 1991, as well as three consecutive RBI titles from 1990-92.

The 1990s brought even more offensive increases, with a variety of reasons at the root of the boom. Not only were the sluggers of the day bigger and stronger, but they also were smarter. Instead of swinging from the heels and trying to pull everything, they took the approach of singles hitters, and took pitches the other way—but with enough power to send them out of the park in any direction.

Pitching was further diluted by two more expansions that brought the number of teams to 30, almost double the longstanding total of 16 that began in the 1900s and lasted until 1961. One of those 1993 expansion teams— the Colorado Rockies—had much to do with the inflation of offensive statistics in the National League simply because they play home games at the mile-high altitude of 5,280 feet in Denver. Thanks to inflated statistics that included run totals about two per game above the league average, Colorado produced three batting champions, three home run champions and three RBI leaders in its first seven years of existence.

Not since the 1910s was there as dramatic a makeover in terms of new stadiums, as teams in Toronto, Chicago, Baltimore, Cleveland, Colorado, Atlanta, and Seattle all opened new parks. Most favored hitters because of cozy dimensions, a

At the turn of the century, the fearsome, game-breaking slugger is back in vogue, as evidenced by the raw power of Frank Thomas (above) and the unlimited potential of Ken Griffey Jr.

lack of foul territory and excellent hitting backgrounds. And even umpires played their part with a stricter interpretation of the strike zone, shrinking it to an area just above to belt to the knees, giving hitters a smaller area to have to protect.

Everybody knows about the captivating 1998 duel with destiny between McGwire and Sammy Sosa, when both surpassed Maris' longstanding mark. And then for good measure, they did it again in 1999 with a sequel that almost measured up to the original. But there was so much more home run hitting of epic proportions as the 20th century came to a close.

Of the 16 times in American League history that a player has hit 50 or more homers in a season, six came in the 1990s: Cecil Fielder (1990), Albert Belle (1995), McGwire and Brady Anderson (1996), and Ken Griffey Jr. (1997 and 1998). Griffey also just missed in both 1996 and 1999, when he hit 49 and 48, giving him a four-year total of 209.

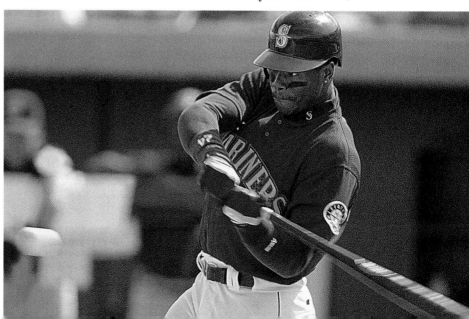

Sammy Sosa might be facing diluted pitching, but there's no denying his power. All eyes are on him when he comes to the plate.

Of the 108 seasons of 40 or more homers in American League history, 39 came in the 1990s.

Belle also had seasons of 49 and 48 homers, and two-time home run champ Juan Gonzalez hit 40 or more five times. Rafael Palmeiro had back-to-back 40-plus homer seasons in 1998 and 1999 and didn't hit fewer than 38 from 1995-1999. Frank Thomas hit 40 or more three times.

Five National League players in addition to McGwire and Sosa hit 40 or more homers in 1999, and Greg Vaughn became only the eighth National League player to hit at least 50 homers in 1998. Of the 12 times that has occurred in the National League, five have come in the last two seasons. Yes, it's bombs away around the big leagues.

"Conditions are different now, namely, the pitching," Reggie Jackson says. "Mark McGwire, Sammy Sosa ... those guys wouldn't have hit 65, 70 homers in a season 25 years ago. Those guys are great home run hitters. Put them in any era, and they would be among the leaders. But they would have been hitting 40 a year, not 60 or 70. McGwire isn't going to hit 65, and Willie Mays hit 38. That's not going to happen. Sammy Sosa is not going to hit 66 homers, and Ernie Banks 45. That's not going to happen. When McGwire hit 70, Sosa hit 66 and two guys hit 50."

How long will the scales be tipped toward hitters? Only the unfolding of a new millennium will tell for certain. But there certainly is a long list of sluggers who are either in their prime or on the verge of it to carry on the slugging tradition into the first part of the 21st century.

Mark McGwire will begin the 2000 season with 522 homers at age 36, and health permitting, has a chance at becoming the third player to hit 700 homers. Ken Griffey Jr. has the best chance to surpass Hank Aaron as the all-time leader, as he is only two homers from 400 at age 30. Alex Rodriguez is on a path to becoming the best slugging shortstop in history, as he already has had two 40-plus homer seasons before his 25th birthday. Manny Ramirez has 198 homers at age 27. Jose Canseco (431) and Barry Bonds (445) will top the 500-homer mark, and Sammy Sosa (336), Albert Belle (338), Juan Gonzalez (340) and Rafael Palmeiro (361) all could get there as well. If so, that would be eight of the top 23 home run hitters of all time from the current generation of sluggers.

What could slow them down? There are a handful of possibilities that could bring about the next shift in dominance, as if nothing else, the game through the years has proved to be cyclical. A return to umpires calling the strike zone as stated in the rule book could make a difference. Major League baseball is in the process of gaining more control of the umpires, but it remains to be seen if strike zone enforcement will be changed.

More new stadiums are on the horizon in Houston, Detroit, Milwaukee, San Francisco, Pittsburgh, San Diego, Cincinnati and Boston. Those possibly could be more pitcher-friendly, as has been the case with the change in venue in Seattle. Artificial turf surfaces, which promote scoring due to balls skipping past infielders and outfielders more rapidly, also are disappearing. St. Louis and Kansas City removed the turf in existing ballparks, Seattle and Houston replaced dome stadiums with retractable-dome parks with grass and Cincinnati also will change from turf to grass.

There always is the possibility of altering the baseball, either by softening it a bit or raising the stitches to help breaking pitches. Ask anybody who has been around the game for a generation or more, and they say the ball is smaller and harder than it used to be. Raising the mound, possibly to its pre-1969 height of 15 inches, or somewhere in between that and the current 10-inch height, is another remedy easily accomplished. And there is plenty of support around the game for the abolishment of the designated hitter in the American League.

Finally, a more-radical idea would be a franchise consolidation due to the growing financial disparities between teams. A fewer number of teams should translate into better overall pitching. But remember that owners also know one pattern that has remained constant throughout the game's history—more offense equals more attendance. So at least for now, offense in general and slugging in particular, is on a bull run paralleling that of Wall Street, and there is no end in sight.

Long live the long ball.

THE FUTURE

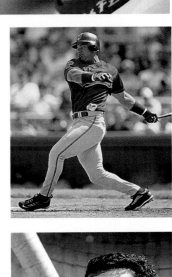

Top row: Ken Griffey Jr., Mark McGwire. Center row: Sammy Sosa, Rafael Palmeiro, Albert Belle, Manny Ramirez. Bottom row: Alex Rodriguez, Juan Gonzalez.

167

FIRST BASE / Mark McGwire

SECOND BASE / Ryne Sandberg

THIRD BASE / Mike Schmidt

Most home runs by position:

Home runs

1.	Hank Aaron	755
2.	Babe Ruth	714
3.	Willie Mays	660
4.	Frank Robinson	586
5.	Harmon Killebrew	573
6.	Reggie Jackson	563
7.	Mike Schmidt	548
8.	Mickey Mantle	536
9.	Jimmie Foxx	534
10.	Mark McGwire	522
11.	Willie McCovey	521
	Ted Williams	521
13.	Ernie Banks	512
	Eddie Mathews	512
15.	Mel Ott	511
16.	Eddie Murray	504
17.	Lou Gehrig	493
18.	Stan Musial	475
	Willie Stargell	475
20.	Dave Winfield	465

Home runs, A.L.

1.	Babe Ruth	708
2.	Harmon Killebrew	573
3.	Reggie Jackson	563
4.	Mickey Mantle	536
5.	Jimmie Foxx	524
6.	Ted Williams	521
7.	Lou Gehrig	493
8.	Carl Yastrzemski	452

9.	Jose Canseco	431
10.	Cal Ripken	402
11.	Al Kaline	399
12.	Ken Griffey Jr.	398
13.	Eddie Murray	396
14.	Dwight Evans	385
15.	Jim Rice	382
16.	Norm Cash	377
17.	Carlton Fisk	376
18.	Harold Baines	373
19.	Rocky Colavito	371
20.	Joe Carter	365

Home runs, N.L.

1.	Hank Aaron	733
2.	Willie Mays	660
3.	Mike Schmidt	548
4.	Willie McCovey	521
5.	Ernie Banks	512
6.	Mel Ott	511
7.	Eddie Mathews	503
8.	Stan Musial	475
	Willie Stargell	475
10.	Barry Bonds	445
11.	Andre Dawson	409
12.	Duke Snider	407
13.	Dale Murphy	398
14.	Billy Williams	392
15.	Johnny Bench	389
16.	Gil Hodges	370
17.	Orlando Cepeda	358

18.	Ralph Kiner	351
19.	George Foster	347
20.	Frank Robinson	343

Home runs, one club

1.	Hank Aaron, Braves	733
2.	Babe Ruth, Yankees	659
3.	Willie Mays, Giants	646
4.	Harmon Killebrew, Senators/Twins	559
5.	Mike Schmidt, Phillies	548
6.	Mickey Mantle, Yankees	536
7.	Ted Williams, Red Sox	521
8.	Ernie Banks, Cubs	512
9.	Mel Ott, Giants	511
10.	Lou Gehrig, Yankees	493
	Eddie Mathews, Braves	493
12.	Stan Musial, Cardinals	475
	Willie Stargell, Pirates	475
14.	Willie McCovey, Giants	469
15.	Carl Yastrzemski, Red Sox	452
16.	Cal Ripken, Orioles	402
17.	Al Kaline, Tigers	399
18.	Ken Griffey Jr., Mariners	398
19.	Billy Williams, Cubs	392
20.	Johnny Bench, Reds	389
	Duke Snider, Dodgers	389

Home runs, righthander

1.	Hank Aaron	755

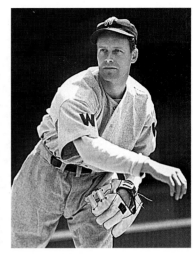

SHORTSTOP / Cal Ripken   **OUTFIELD / Babe Ruth**   **CATCHER / Carlton Fisk**   **PITCHER / Wes Ferrell**

2.	Willie Mays	660
3.	Frank Robinson	586
4.	Harmon Killebrew	573
5.	Mike Schmidt	548
6.	Jimmie Foxx	534
7.	Mark McGwire	522
8.	Ernie Banks	512
9.	Dave Winfield	465
10.	Dave Kingman	442
11.	Andre Dawson	438
12.	Jose Canseco	431
13.	Cal Ripken	402
14.	Al Kaline	399
15.	Dale Murphy	398
16.	Joe Carter	396
17.	Johnny Bench	389
18.	Dwight Evans	385
19.	Frank Howard	382
	Jim Rice	382

Home runs, lefthander

1.	Babe Ruth	714
2.	Reggie Jackson	563
3.	Willie McCovey	521
	Ted Williams	521
5.	Eddie Mathews	512
6.	Mel Ott	511
7.	Lou Gehrig	493
8.	Stan Musial	475
	Willie Stargell	475
10.	Carl Yastrzemski	452

11.	Barry Bonds	445
12.	Billy Williams	426
13.	Darrell Evans	414
14.	Duke Snider	407
15.	Ken Griffey Jr.	398
16.	Fred McGriff	390
	Graig Nettles	390
18.	Norm Cash	377
19.	Harold Baines	373
20.	Rafael Palmeiro	361

Home runs, switch hitter

1.	Mickey Mantle	536
2.	Eddie Murray	504
3.	Chili Davis	350
4.	Reggie Smith	314
5.	Bobby Bonilla	277
6.	Ted Simmons	248
7.	Ken Singleton	246
8.	Mickey Tettleton	245
9.	Ruben Sierra	239
10.	Howard Johnson	228
11.	Ken Caminiti	209
12.	Devon White	190
13.	Tim Raines	168
14.	Roy Smalley	163
15.	Tony Phillips	160
	Pete Rose	160
	Roy White	160
18.	Chipper Jones	153
	Tom Tresh	153

| 20. | Roberto Alomar | 151 |
| | Bernie Williams | 151 |

Home runs, first baseman

1.	Mark McGwire	507
2.	Lou Gehrig	493
3.	Jimmie Foxx	480
4.	Willie McCovey	439
5.	Eddie Murray	409
6.	Norm Cash	367
7.	Johnny Mize	350
8.	Fred McGriff	344
9.	Gil Hodges	335
10.	Andres Galarraga	331

Home runs, second baseman

1.	Ryne Sandberg	275
2.	Joe Morgan	266
3.	Rogers Hornsby	264
4.	Joe Gordon	246
5.	Lou Whitaker	239
6.	Bobby Doerr	223
7.	Bobby Grich	196
8.	Charley Gehringer	181
9.	Frank White	156
10.	Tony Lazzeri	149

Home runs, third baseman

1.	Mike Schmidt	509
2.	Eddie Mathews	486
3.	Graig Nettles	368

4.	Ron Santo	337
5.	Gary Gaetti	333
6.	Matt Williams	315
7.	Ron Cey	312
8.	Brooks Robinson	266
9.	Ken Boyer	260
10.	Tim Wallach	249

Home runs, shortstop

1.	Cal Ripken	345
2.	Ernie Banks	277
3.	Vern Stephens	213
4.	Alan Trammell	177
5.	Barry Larkin	166
6.	Joe Cronin	155
7.	Alex Rodriguez	148
8.	Eddie Joost	129
9.	Rico Petrocelli	127
10.	Pee Wee Reese	122
	Robin Yount	122

Home runs, outfielder

1.	Babe Ruth	692
2.	Hank Aaron	661
3.	Willie Mays	642
4.	Ted Williams	514
5.	Mickey Mantle	490
6.	Frank Robinson	463
7.	Reggie Jackson	458
8.	Mel Ott	457
9.	Barry Bonds	442
10.	Andre Dawson	404

Home runs, catcher

1.	Carlton Fisk	351
2.	Johnny Bench	327
3.	Yogi Berra	306
4.	Gary Carter	298
5.	Lance Parrish	295
6.	Roy Campanella	239
7.	Mike Piazza	237

8.	Gabby Hartnett	232
9.	Bill Dickey	200
10.	Ted Simmons	195

Home runs, pitcher

1.	Wes Ferrell	37
2.	Bob Lemon	35
	Warren Spahn	35
4.	Red Ruffing	34
5.	Earl Wilson	33
6.	Don Drysdale	29
7.	John Clarkson	24
	Bob Gibson	24
9.	Walter Johnson	23
10.	Jack Stivetts	20
	Dizzy Trout	20

Home runs, designated hitter

1.	Don Baylor	219
2.	Harold Baines	203
3.	Chili Davis	200
4.	Jose Canseco	179
5.	Hal McRae	145

Leadoff homers

1.	Rickey Henderson	75
2.	Brady Anderson	36
3.	Bobby Bonds	35
4.	Paul Molitor	33
5.	Devon White	31
6.	Tony Phillips	30
7.	Davey Lopes	28
	Eddie Yost	28
9.	Chuck Knoblauch	27
10.	Brian Downing	25
11.	Lou Brock	24
12.	Tommy Harper	23
	Lou Whitaker	23
14.	Jimmy Ryan	22
15.	Craig Biggio	21
16.	Felipe Alou	20

	Barry Bonds	20
	Lenny Dykstra	20
19.	Eddie Joost	19
	Dick McAuliffe	19

20-home run seasons

1.	Hank Aaron	20
2.	Willie Mays	17
	Frank Robinson	17
4.	Reggie Jackson	16
	Eddie Murray	16
	Babe Ruth	16
	Ted Williams	16
8.	Mel Ott	15
	Willie Stargell	15
	Dave Winfield	15
11.	Mickey Mantle	14
	Eddie Mathews	14
	Mike Schmidt	14
	Billy Williams	14
15.	Ernie Banks	13
	Andre Dawson	13
	Lou Gehrig	13
	Harmon Killebrew	13
19.	10 tied with 12	

30-home run seasons

1.	Hank Aaron	15
2.	Babe Ruth	13
	Mike Schmidt	13
4.	Jimmie Foxx	12
5.	Willie Mays	11
	Frank Robinson	11
7.	Lou Gehrig	10
	Harmon Killebrew	10
	Eddie Mathews	10
	Mark McGwire	10
11.	Barry Bonds	9
	Mickey Mantle	9
13.	Albert Belle	8
	Jose Canseco	8

	Fred McGriff	8
	Mel Ott	8
	Ted Williams	8
18.	Ernie Banks	7
	Rocky Colavito	7
	Joe DiMaggio	7
	Reggie Jackson	7
	Ralph Kiner	7
	Dave Kingman	7
	Willie McCovey	7

Ballparks hitting home runs

1.	Fred McGriff	36
2.	Ellis Burks	34
	Gary Gaetti	34
	Mark McGwire	34
5.	Devon White	33
6.	Joe Carter	32
	Roger Connor	32
	Chili Davis	32
	Eddie Murray	32
	Frank Robinson	32
	Rusty Staub	32
	Harry Stovey	32
	Dave Winfield	32
14.	Hank Aaron	31
15.	Ron Fairly	30
	Kirk Gibson	30
	Pete Incaviglia	30
	Al Oliver	30
	Paul O'Neill	30
	Gary Sheffield	30

Pinch-hit home runs

1.	Cliff Johnson	20
2.	Jerry Lynch	18
3.	Gates Brown	16
	Smoky Burgess	16
	Willie McCovey	16
6.	George Crowe	14
7.	John Vander Wal	13

8.	Joe Adcock	12
	Bob Cerv	12
	Jose Morales	12
	Graig Nettles	12
12.	Jeff Burroughs	11
	Jay Johnstone	11
	Candy Maldonado	11
	Fred Whitfield	11
	Cy Williams	11
17.	11 tied with 10	

Grand slams

1.	Lou Gehrig	23
2.	Eddie Murray	19
3.	Willie McCovey	18
4.	Jimmie Foxx	17
	Ted Williams	17
6.	Hank Aaron	16
	Dave Kingman	16
	Babe Ruth	16
9.	Gil Hodges	14
10.	Harold Baines	13
	Joe DiMaggio	13
	George Foster	13
	Ralph Kiner	13
	Mark McGwire	13
	Robin Ventura	13
16.	Ernie Banks	12
	Don Baylor	12
	Ken Griffey Jr.	12
	Rogers Hornsby	12
	Joe Rudi	12
	Rudy York	12

Multiple-home run games

1.	Babe Ruth	72
2.	Willie Mays	63
3.	Hank Aaron	62
	Mark McGwire	62
5.	Jimmie Foxx	55
6.	Frank Robinson	54

7.	Eddie Mathews	49
	Mel Ott	49
9.	Harmon Killebrew	46
	Mickey Mantle	46
11.	Willie McCovey	44
	Mike Schmidt	44
13.	Dave Kingman	43
14.	Ernie Banks	42
	Barry Bonds	42
	Lou Gehrig	42
	Reggie Jackson	42
18.	Ken Griffey Jr.	40
	Ralph Kiner	40
20.	Andre Dawson	39
	Sammy Sosa	39

Most homers per at-bat

1.	Mark McGwire	.092
2.	Babe Ruth	.085
3.	Ralph Kiner	.071
4.	Juan Gonzalez	.070
	Harmon Killebrew	.070
6.	Ken Griffey Jr.	.068
	Albert Belle	.068
	Ted Williams	.068
9.	Jose Canseco	.067
10.	Dave Kingman	.066
	Mickey Mantle	.066
	Mike Piazza	.066
	Jimmie Foxx	.066
	Mike Schmidt	.066
15.	Barry Bonds	.064
	Hank Greenberg	.064
	Willie McCovey	.064
	Sammy Sosa	.064
19.	Cecil Fielder	.062
	Darryl Strawberry	.062

Selecting the proper bat was probably as difficult for Roger Maris, Ted Williams and Mickey Mantle as it was for our editors to select baseball's 50 greatest sluggers.

The process for selecting and ranking

the 50 Greatest Sluggers was both a quantitative and qualitative endeavor. Members of THE SPORTING NEWS staff combed through a number of statistics—total home runs, slugging percentage, home runs per at-bat, total bases and a combination of those statistics—and they considered, simply, the perception of players as sluggers.

Included in our presentation of each slugger, you'll find a TSNdex power ranking, produced with the help of Dr. Don Guthrie, a professor emeritus at UCLA who has a degree in statistics from Stanford. The power ranking is a number derived by a statistical formula that considered doubles, triples, home runs, runs batted in and slugging, among players with a minimum of six years and 600 at-bats.

On a project such as this, there are always a number of people who pitched in and made it happen.

So, to the team who helped select and rank the players—Chris Bahr, Craig Carter, Mark Bonavita, Tony DeMarco, Steve Gietschier, Jared Hoffman, Joe Hoppel, Michael Knisley, Bill Ladson, Jim Meier, John Rawlings, Bob Parajon, Brendan Roberts, Dave Sloan and Ron Smith—thanks for the hours of time and energy you gave to careful consideration of the thousands of players from which we had to choose; to our design and production team—Bob Parajon, Bill Wilson and Michael Behrens, thanks for your creativity and attention to detail to make this book as eye-popping as it is; to our prepress team of Dave Brickey, Jack Kruyne and Steve Romer, whose skills can make the worst of images a work of art.

To Paul Nisely, whose contacts and sources turned up the incredible images in this book, and for the countless hours it took gathering, editing and organizing those images; to Steve Gietschier and Jim Meier, whose research and fact-checking should never be overlooked or underappreciated; to Ron Smith, who provided advice and counsel throughout the project; to John Rawlings and Kathy Kinkeade, thanks for allocating the support and necessary resources to pull this project together; to everyone at The Sporting News, who picked up other work and allowed this project to continue.

Over-and-above thanks must go out to two people—Tony DeMarco and Leslie Gibson McCarthy— former colleagues and forever friends who researched, wrote and edited this project.

One final acknowledgement. Baseball statistics can be a moving target. Some organizations recognize some numbers; other organizations recognize different numbers. For the sake of consistency, our reference for all statistics in this book was Total Baseball.

Steve Meyerhoff
Executive Editor
The Sporting News

Photo credits

Contents: Kluszewski (Corbis/Bettman-UPI); Title Page: Maris (Corbis/Bettman-UPI); Introduction: Ruth (Photofile), Jackson (Malcolm W. Emmons), McGwire (Robert Seale/TSN), McGwire and Sosa (Ed Nessen/TSN). McGwire (Ed Nessen/TSN), Maris (TSN Archives), Mantle (TSN Archives); 1) Ruth: left to right: (Charles Conlon/TSN Archives), (TSN Archives), (TSN Archives); 2) McGwire: left to right: (Dilip Vishwanat/TSN), (Robert Seale/TSN), (Dilip Vishwanat/TSN), (TSN Archives); 3) Foxx: left to right: (Corbis/Bettman-UPI), (TSN Archives); 4) Mantle: Mantle and Stengel (TSN Archives), left to right: (Tony Tomsic), (TSN Archives); 5) Aaron: left to right: (Malcolm W. Emmons), (Photofile); 6) Mays: left to right: (Malcolm W. Emmons), (Corbis/Bettman-UPI); 7) Killebrew: left to right: (Malcolm W. Emmons), (TSN Archives); 8) Jackson: left to right: (Malcolm W. Emmons), (Photofile); 9) McCovey: left to right: (Malcolm W. Emmons), (TSN Archives), (Photofile); 10) Schmidt: left to right: (Michael Ponzini), (Rick Stewart/Allsport); 11) Williams: left to right: (Corbis/Bettman-UPI), (Corbis/Bettman-UPI), (TSN Archives); 12) Griffey: left to right: (Vincent Laforet/Allsport), (Dilip Vishwanat/TSN); 13) Gehrig: left to right: (Corbis/Bettman-UPI), (Photofile); 14) Kiner: left to right: (TSN Archives), (Photofile); 15) Greenberg: left to right: (TSN Archives), (TSN Archives); 16) Robinson: left to right: (TSN Archives), (Malcolm W. Emmons); 17) Mathews: left to right: (Photofile), Mathews and Aaron (TSN Archives); 18) Howard: left to right: (Tony Tomsic), (Malcolm W. Emmons); 19) Canseco: left to right: (TSN Archives), (TSN Archives); 20) Ott: left to right: (TSN Archives), (TSN Archives), (Corbis/Bettman-UPI); 21) Sosa: left to right: (TSN Archives), (Photofile), (Steve Woltman For TSN); 22) Stargell: left to right: (Photofile), (Tony Tomsic), (Michael Ponzini), (Malcolm W. Emmons); 23) Colavito: left to right: (Photofile), (Tony Tomsic); 24) DiMaggio: left to right: (Photofile), (Corbis/Bettman-UPI); 25) Musial: left to right: (TSN Archives), (Photofile), (TSN Archives); 26) Mize: left to right: (TSN Archives), (TSN Archives), (Corbis/Bettman-UPI); 27) Snider: (TSN Archives); 28) Belle: left to right: (Jonathan Daniel/Allsport), (TSN Archives), (Bob Leverone/TSN); 29) Bonds: left to right: (TSN Archives), (TSN Archives), (TSN Archives); 30) Gonzalez: left to right: (TSN Archives), (Stephen Dunn/Allsport), (John McConnico for TSN); 31) Fielder: left to right: (TSN Archives), (TSN Archives); 32) Kingman: left to right: (Jonathan Daniel/Allsport), (J. Rettaliata/Allsport); 33) Wilson: left to right: (Corbis/Bettman-UPI), (Corbis/Bettman-UPI), (TSN Archives); 34) Banks: left to right: (Malcolm W. Emmons), (TSN Archives), (Photofile); 35) Maris: left to right: (Corbis/Bettman-UPI), (Corbis/Bettman-UPI), (Photofile); 36) Allen: left to right: (Malcolm W. Emmons); 37) Luzinski: left to right: (Harold Moon/TSN Archives), (Malcolm W. Emmons), (Ed Mailliard/TSN Archives); 38) Kluszewski: left to right: (TSN Archives), (TSN Archives); 39) Thomas: left to right: (TSN Archives), (TSN Archives), (Robert Seale/TSN); 40) Bench: left to right: (Tony Tomsic), (Malcolm W. Emmons); 41) Klein: left to right: (TSN Archives), (Corbis/Bettman-UPI); 42) Powell: left to right: (Malcolm W. Emmons), (Photofile); 43) Rice: left to right: (TSN Archives), (Peter Travers/TSN Archives), (TSN Archives); 44) Foster: left to right: (Malcolm W. Emmons), (TSN Archives), (Peter Travers/TSN Archives); 45) Winfield: left to right: (Corbis/Bettman-UPI), (TSN Archives); 46) Murray: left to right: (Doug Pensinger/Allsport), (TSN Archives), (TSN Archives); 47) Dawson: left to right: (TSN Archives), (TSN Archives), (TSN Archives); 48) Yastrzemski: left to right: (Malcolm W. Emmons), Yastrzemski and Williams (TSN Archives), (Malcolm W. Emmons); 49) Murphy: left to right: (TSN Archives), (TSN Archives), (TSN Archives); 50) McGriff: left to right: (Albert Dickson/TSN), (Ed Nessen/TSN), (TSN Archives); Pre-1900: Spread (Charles Conlon/TSN Archives), Circle (TSN Archives), Keeler (TSN Archives), Both McGraw (TSN Archives), Lowe (TSN Archives), Anson (Corbis/Bettman-UPI), Duffy (TSN Archives), Delahanty (TSN Archives), Burkett (TSN Archives); 1900-1918: Spread (Charles Conlon/TSN Archives). Circle (TSN Archives). Baker (TSN Archives), Crawford (TSN Archives), Cravath (TSN Archives), Johnson (TSN Archives), Christy (TSN Archives), Young (TSN Archives), Zimmerman (TSN Archives), Cobb (Charles Conlon/TSN Archives), Honus (TSN Archives), Shibe (Charles Conlon/TSN Archives); 1919-1942: Spread (Charles Conlon/TSN Archives), Circle (Photofile), Ruth Hall of Fame (TSN Archives), Ruth (TSN Archives). Hornsby (TSN Archives), Heilmann (TSN Archives), Gehrig and Ruth (TSN Archives), Foxx (TSN Archives), Ott (TSN Archives), Klein (TSN Archives), Wilson (TSN Archives), Greeenberg (TSN Archives), Gibson (TSN Archives), Leonard (Negro League Baseball Museum Inc.); 1943-1968: Spread (TSN Archives), Circle (TSN Archives), Kiner (TSN Archives), Kluszewski (Photofile), Kiner (TSN Archives), Mays (Malcolm W. Emmons), Mantle (Louis Requena), Snider (TSN Archives), Aaron (Malcolm W. Emmons), Robinson (Tony Tomsic), Killebrew (Tony Tomsic), Matthews (TSN Archives), Mantle and Maris (Corbis/Bettman-UPI), Maris 61 (Corbis/Bettman-UPI), Yastrzemski (Malcolm W. Emmons); 1969-Present: Spread (TSN Archives), Circle (Albert Dickson/TSN). Torre (TSN Archives), Rico (Jay Spencer/TSN Archives), Winfield (TSN Archives), Murray (TSN Archives), Blomberg (TSN Archives), Jackson (Tony Tomsic), Schmidt (Michael Ponzini), Foster (Malcolm W. Emmons), Allen (Malcolm W. Emmons), Brett (TSN Archives), Canseco and McGwire (Albert Dickson/TSN), Fielder (TSN Archives), Thomas (TSN Archives), Griffey (TSN Archives), Sosa (Ed Nessen/TSN); Future: Griffey (Bob Leverone/TSN), McGwire (Dilip Vishwanat/TSN), Sosa (Ed Nessen/TSN), Palmiero (Dilip Vishwanat/TSN), Belle (Bob Leverone/TSN), Ramirez (John Dunn for TSN), Rodriguez (Dilip Vishwanat/TSN), Gonzalez (Dilip Vishwanat/TSN); HR Leaders: McGwire (Albert Dickson/TSN), Sandberg (TSN Archives), Schmidt (TSN Archives), Ripken (Bob Leverone/TSN), Ruth (TSN Archives), Fisk (TSN Archives), Ferrel (TSN Archives), Williams, Maris and Mantle (TSN Archives)

ISBN: 0-89204-632-5

10 9 8 7 6 5 4 3 2 1